BLACK

JOY

UNBOUND

An Anthology

BLACK

JOY

UNBOUND

An Anthology

PRESS

Bloomington | Clayton

Printed in the United States of America

First Printing, 2023

Cover art and design: Lauren Curry

Paperback ISBN-13: 978-1-7359065-5-3

Library of Congress Control Number: 2023943494

BLF Press
PO Box 8451
Bloomington, IN 47407

www.blfpress.com

CONTENTS

For those who struggle
to find joy, and for those
who revel in it.

Recently
Triston Dabney

I find myself setting a fire
of laughter and front teeth
at the sounds of children.
I see the path of God
within our smile lines.

I find myself crying at
every song and wave,
As does an infant
discovering life for the first time,
As though a caveman
who has just now rendered heat
from his own fire.

If I could give it a name,
This existent joy,
I'd call it "Maya,"
My soul now stretching as I rise.

peppa
for Grandma Rosie
Whitney French

let yourself get lost in the rhythm
—free up, like double dutch where

timing meets teamwork, my feet
favah peppa, in rhythm

of dollar store plastic pink
slapping black off hot

tarmac, back into heartbeat
consistency, choosing wonder

as lifestyle, as rhythm
made by hands of budding Black girls

this requires a level of faith;
nothing more holy than honey-fallen

blessings, heavy on melanated knees
synching verses to the song of rope.

It Shines Within Us
Tiffany Smalls

I find it in the peach tree outside my aunt's house,
the spot my uncles used to play basketball
with a wicker basket. Find it in the harmonies
of the past, when we were young
dreamers, unafraid of our voices being heard.
It's in the bass booming as a 90s throwback
shakes the car. It's in our laughter, remembering
how we used to whisper the cuss words
when our parents weren't around.
It's in the euphoria of someone speaking how you do,
pull out the Carmex and Blue Magic,
pick their fro out like you do.
It's staying in the summer sun, splashing
in the public pool. It's syrup-dripping popsicles
and dollar pizza slices, before a bike ride home.
It's seeing your face in your baby niece's smile.
Even in the dark, it's there in our blood,
in the lineage that birthed us,
it pounds in our hearts like a never-ending
drum: the 808s of happiness
and a beat drop of joy.

Three Years Later
A. Brown

Even in the summers, we all got up at eight in the morning to catch Mommy's daily phone call. Crime didn't take a break and neither did public defenders, so she spent the weeks in Richmond, even when we had nothing to do all day but miss her. We crowded around the off-white wall phone and waited impatiently for our turn to say, "Mommy, guess what?" And she'd still sound interested, no matter how mundane the news.

While it took her three hours to get to Richmond from Jubilant City at the start of the week, it only took twenty-five minutes to get back. That was part of the city's charm I had come to learn, it was close by if needed. We'd visited her office once: a room made up of four walls, a bulletin board, a desk covered in stacks of too-full folders and more humidity than the deep South. She glowed as she gave us the grand tour, describing everything that she loved so much about her chair, the carpet, the fluorescent lights, the baseboards.

Our family lived on the outskirts of the city in an area called The Crick, for the skinny trail of water that formed a border between our neighborhood and Little Village. Little Village was the oasis and The Crick was the inferno. Little Village took all the heart and fun from downtown JC and painted it pastel, turned down the noise and pointed it's pinky. I had never seen a green lawn in The Crick, but they were all over Little Village. While we lived in shacks and houses, the people of Little Village lived in cabins and bungalows. Commissioned an artist to sculpt their own tree that they placed in the middle of a roundabout. The Crick was the farthest neighborhood from the center tree that gave the city its magic, which meant we got the scraps. The misshapen and defunct magic. Men that claimed to have sucked sap from the tree for the teas and elixirs they sold. Said all we had to do was drink and the city would give us the life we wanted.

But Daddy had none of it. Always said if life was about getting what we want then we'd already have it. He had inherited our house and its three bedrooms from Granny, his momma. When I was young we moved in and Granny taught me how to play the dozens. "Emmanuel and Erica Jr. are winning because you don't know better, but I'll teach you." The next time Erica Jr. called me a tattletale, I talked right back to her about her halitosis breath and to Emmanuel about his constantly cracking voice that made him sound like a cartoon character, even though he was trying to get Erica Jr. off me. After that, Granny taught me about friendly fire.

It was the hottest part of the summer and the first time since I could remember, my day started with silence. Erica Jr. wasn't playing her radio too loud in the bathroom, Moses wasn't rifling through the clean clothes for a pair of underwear. And Emmanuel wasn't doing jumping jacks or the push ups with claps in between. By the time I emerged from our little house, in a rush, my house dress skewed on my body, something didn't feel right. I walked into the sun that hissed moisture from the asphalt and knelt next to the underspot of our small front porch. The house next to ours was home to a man that played the piano at one of the churches in Little Village. We never saw him leave without dropping every piece of sheet music he needed for the day. Once, Emmanuel had helped gather them, stepped on one to keep it from blowing away. The man ain't like that too much, snatched it from Emmanuel and flipped him the bird. "Y'all see that man lose his music, you let it happen," he told us afterward, Daddy nodding in silence.

On the other side, my classmate, Bianca, stayed with her mom and little sister. Erica Jr. and I were sure that all they did was think of new ways to make us miserable, like pointing out the ash that sometimes touched my kneecaps. Granny always said she felt sorry for her. "Little girl ain't never got her hair done. Always wearing dirty clothes while her Momma got on designer. A damn shame."

I felt my hand around the soft dirt until it landed firmly on a small box. I spread my fingers across the top, feeling for the gentle scudding of wings brushing against it from underneath. I felt nothing.

Emmanuel and Daddy pulled up in the truck and told me that I missed Mommy's phone call. They went out every morning and picked up people in The Crick, taking them into JC to work. Most days it was only two or three people, but those two or three people wouldn't be able to get to work any other way. Daddy didn't want anyone else to ruin their back like Granny did. Trekking up the street each morning forced her back into a round curve. She didn't even look comfortable in her coffin.

"Why ain't you wake me up?" I called to them, wiping the dirt from the box to reveal the delicate leaf pattern embossed into the lid.

"Why wasn't you down here with the rest of us?" Emmanuel had our father's face and our mother's temperament—and her nose. When she was in Richmond, Emmanuel was our family's steady hand. He'd been out of high school for a couple of years, but stuck around and fixed bikes and air conditioners and refrigerators for people in The Crick while he figured out the rest of his life.

"That just ain't fair. Erica Jr. kept me up all night—"

"Doing what?" Daddy hopped out of the truck, sweat covering his forehead. His head was balding in a straight line down the middle, from his forehead to his crown. When it was cool enough for a hat, he usually went with a cowboy hat that my little brother, Moses, and I got him for Father's Day.

I zipped my lip because Erica Jr. hadn't given me permission to tell that she snuck a few phone calls on the landline the night before. She always hid behind the couch, just in case Daddy or Emmanuel got up for a drink. Emmanuel looked like someone put my momma's nose on my daddy's face and called that good, while Erica Jr. looked like my momma had made her all by herself. She'd inherited her five-foot frame, her halo of kinky hair, and the beauty mark she wore on her chin. Like my daddy, Emmanuel was mostly harmless, but I feared Erica Jr.'s wrath like I feared dentist appointments.

Emmanuel sucked his teeth, "On that phone."

"I'ma split that girl's head with a rock," Daddy said. His threats were nothing if not empty; he was never one for spanking. He much preferred making fun of you for attempting to do wrong at all. *Them A's you get in school don't mean a thing if you can't learn the most valuable lesson: I can't be fooled.*

"You just need to make sure you up on time, Puddin'." Emmanuel pulled a large bag of fish from the back of the cab, the price scribbled lazily on the label. The bag of whiskered fish made me want to gag, all four sets of eyes were pressed against the base of the bag. Each fish was more surprised than the last about where he'd ended up. Emmanuel wiggled his eyebrows, "Dinner." He handed the bag to daddy and headed over to the mailbox at the end of the lawn.

"What about lunch?" Daddy dangled the bag in front of my face and I pushed it away.

"You on your own for lunch. Now go play and don't keep runnin' in and out my house."

Daddy went inside and Emmanuel walked to the edge of the yard, looking up and down the street like he was waiting for the bus. I turned my attention back to the box, gently pulling off the lid. Inside, the origami butterflies folded into dangerously thin squares of paper laid dead in the box.

"What's today?" I called to Emmanuel, shaking the box gently as I made my way across the yard.

"The seventeenth," he said, still turning his head side to side like a rooster wind vane in a dry breeze.

It was July seventeenth. The butterflies were supposed to come alive on July the 17th just like they had the year before. And the year before. But even though I'd kept them buried and untouched like I was supposed to, they hadn't come back to life.

"You got this, Mo!" Emmanuel yelled suddenly through

21

Three Years Later

cupped hands. My little brother, Moses, ran as fast as his legs would take him up the street toward the house. He had my bookbag on his back and his own bag on his front, both full of books and making him look twice his size.

When he arrived he yanked off the bags and nearly folded his body in half as he leaned over, huffing and puffing. Beads of sweat raced down his face like raindrops on a window.

"How you feel, champ?" Emmanuel bounced on his toes and tossed two play jabs at the empty air above Moses' head.

"Tired."

"I know, but while you *flying* to the finish line, them other kids will be whining about their legs hurting. And you know why that is? Because you did your training."

Moses shook his head, still breathing too hard to speak. He only had a couple of hours before all the other fifth graders lined up on the corner of Sherman and Washington for The Race. Winner got a bike and Moses knew he wouldn't get one for Christmas this year, Daddy said it just wasn't in the Lord's plan this time around. The house that had held up so well over the years had begun falling apart. Most of Daddy's time was spent fixing this or that or getting prices for a new something versus just getting a used something and weighing the benefits of having a friend or Emmanuel help him versus just taking care of it himself. "Next Christmas," he promised. But Moses couldn't wait for next Christmas. He was almost eleven. By the next Christmas he'd be twelve and too old to learn to ride a bike for the first time. And *that*? That would be the end of the world.

"Y'all seen anybody else practicing?" Moses' voice was breathy and scant. He wiped his face with the collar of his shirt.

"Nah," I said. "It's the seventeenth."

Moses' eyes settled on the box in my hands. He was the only one I'd told about the butterflies because I thought he missed grandma like I did. When she died our mother had simply told him that she'd gone away. He took the time to draw up missing posters with our address and phone number and Emmanuel took him out to hang them. But a box of flying paper butterflies was where he drew the line.

"Stop lying," he'd said. "You always making stuff up." Granny'd called it "embellishing," but made it clear that I needed to grow out of it. Quickly. Three years later and I was still working on it. Most of my family just refused to believe me about anything surprising unless I had a witness.

Emmanuel grabbed the bookbags from the ground, "Get your breath, then take another lap."

Moses found his voice, "*Another* lap?"

Emmanuel dropped the bags to the ground. He put his hands on his hips and jutted his stomach out like an assistant coach. "When I was in cross country I ran fifteen *keelomeeters* a race. You know how much I had to practice? I had to get up at four in the morning. I ran before school *and* after school. And I don't even have a bike to show for it. I *thank* you got it easy."

Moses wiped his face again, "Ew, you sound just like Daddy."

Emmanuel smirked, "And I'ma go and get him unless you take another lap. I'll tell him you half assin' it."

Three Years Later

Good thing for Moses, the only person more competitive than Daddy was up in Richmond for the week.

Moses let out a huff and took off down the street again. Emmanuel turned on his heel and walked in the house. As I watched Moses look over his shoulder before slowing to a trot, the heat rising off the asphalt making him look warped and blurry, I thought of Granny and the stash of lidocaine she kept in the medicine cabinet. Long after my daddy moved out and started his own family, she still trekked to JC to volunteer at the school she'd taught art at for thirty-five years. We moved into her house to help before Moses, but after me. The house where she'd raised my daddy and his other siblings.

Me, Erica Jr., and Granny shared the large open bedroom on the ground floor, our beds tucked in opposite corners. We used to crowd around her, keeping a close watch on her every move. Despite her shaking hands, Granny did our hair every morning and made sure that our school clothes were creased in the right places. Rubbed our legs and arms down with petroleum jelly after every bath. Taught us to catch flies out of the air with our bare hands and to make a hair pudding that cleared ringworm, dandruff, and anything else that made the scalp itch.

Origami was what me and grandma did together, just the two of us. She dug up pictures of her old work. A paper swan the size of an end table. An elephant three or four inches taller than she was. And a paper boat durable enough to hold her and a two-year-old version of my daddy on a short sail down the creek. She knew three ways to fold a butterfly into a sheet of paper and she'd taught me every single one.

She'd found a special kind of paper, one that felt and looked more like thin yellow lace. We filled the box with our folds, making sure each crease was perfect. Eventually Grandma resigned to making the larger initial pairs and letting me take care of all of the details.

"I have a surprise for you," she'd said when the box was finally full and safe beneath the porch. "I'll give it to you on my birthday."

When I dug out the box on her birthday, the top rattled, the buzz of wings threatening to rip it in half. When I pulled off the lid, they poured out in a strong storm and then wrapped around me. Bright yellow wings flitted, lapping against the summer air. They took their time filing neatly back into the box, falling into neat and tiny rows. Their wings jittered and, eventually, fell silent.

Years later my momma would tell me that Granny knew I needed a little extra care. That in a house with so many big personalities, one of us was bound to slip through the cracks.

I missed her.

During the week, while Momma was out, Daddy turned the dining room into his own construction zone. Tools spread across the dining room table, broken car parts and pieces of whatever reserved spots at the table. He brought boxes up from the basement just to dig through them and move on. We usually ate dinner crossed legged on the floor, crowded around the TV set.

"Just sit your little box down and help me clear a spot

to fix up this fish."

"I thought you said it was for dinner."

"It is. I gotta filet 'em and debone 'em and Moses' race is at noon. C'mon, move this right here."

I left the box in the safety of the living room and moved a stack of repair manuals onto the floor. Daddy would find a way to hide everything around the house before Momma came back for the weekend.

He pulled the large bag of fish on the table, "I know you can't hold water." He ripped open the bag and dumped the family of fish into the large bowl on the table. "But I'll tell you anyway. Your momma's pregnant."

"Pregnant?"

"Mhm."

"Where's that baby gonna go? We're already bustin' outta here like biscuits, Daddy."

Daddy smirked, tossing equal parts cornmeal and cornstarch into a large disposable baking pan. "Well, Emmanuel's on his way out the door damn near. Erica Jr.'s not far behind."

"Can't we just enjoy having a house that's half empty then?"

"'Fraid not."

When the new baby came, I'd be right in the middle. Two on either side of me, like the wheels on the trailer we'd probably be sleeping in if they kept popping them out. "I'm done?" Daddy had begun chopping the heads off of the fish; every now and then a tail would flop and he'd smack it with the flat part of his knife.

"Yeah, get on outta here."

"You better be nice to me, Daddy," I said. "I know your secret."

Daddy picked up one of the fish heads so that it was looking right at me. He pinched its mouth and said, "So? Won't nobody believe you anyway."

Only Erica Jr. remembered when Emmanuel was short and skinny and mean. Me and Moses only knew him as a tall, de facto parent. He sat us all down for dinner on time every night. Took me over to Little Village when he'd heard one of the boys pushed me (Emmanuel held him down while I got my lick back too). We were watching him turn into our father right in front of us, but a few inches taller.

Emmanuel and Moses had completely transformed the big room on the ground floor since me and Erica Jr. moved to the smaller one upstairs. They'd pushed both of the beds together, making one large spread where Emmanuel slept spread eagle with his mouth wide open. Moses preferred sleeping on the large cushions from a couch Daddy had thrown out years ago. In one corner of the room Emmanuel had stacked his tools, spare bike parts and shop towels. Moses had a stack of books, a bundle of blankets, underwear, other clean clothes, and a stash of empty potato chip bags stuffed beneath his pillow.

"Daddy said what now?" Emmanuel was hunched over an old rusted toolbox where he kept his money. Several bills rolled tight and held together with rubber bands. I had never seen Emmanuel spend a dime.

I took a deep breath, "To give me fifty cents to get a

snack from the store for lunch."

He looked at me over his shoulder, "You *know* you a lie. Daddy just bought all that fish, he not finna spend no money on snacks for you." Though he wanted to be upset, he just shook his head and handed me a crumpled dollar bill. "Take this one. I don't like when they got too many rips anyway. Next time just ask. *Don't* lie."

I took the dollar and left the room.

Emmanuel called up the hallway, "And be back by noon!"

I walked outside and past Erica Jr. and her friends pretending to be Destiny's Child on the side of the house and headed to the corner store.

It looked incomplete, sitting right on the corner of two streets with no other buildings. It looked like someone had squeezed a store into a single cube of an ice tray. The shelves were cramped, but organized, with all of the expensive items in the middle, the cheap stuff at the bottom and extra stock up at the top. There was a deep freezer up at the counter that looked just like the one we had at home, packed with ice cream bars, rocket pops and homemade snow cones. It was run by a woman and her husband—sometimes. She sold colorful scarves that she kept behind the counter and burned incense that she stuck between the layers of peeling paint in the front door jamb.

I gave her the crumpled money and plucked a can of soda and a bag of Lays from the display just below the front counter. She took the money in her fist, then she turned it over and opened it to reveal two shiny quarters. She gave me a toothy grin.

I thanked her and hurried outside to the payphone perched just outside of the shade from the store's awning. I wiped the dirt from the smooth cage the phone sat in and carefully sat down the soda, chips, and box. I pushed in a quarter and dialed Momma's office number. She'd made sure we memorized it the day she got that job. We couldn't talk to her all the time. "But call and leave a message with my secretary and we'll talk all about it when I come home."

I expected her secretary to pick up, but instead the phone just rang and rang. I passed a look up and down the street, hung up, pushed in the other quarter, dialed again. The tone began to sound like white noise I'd heard it so much. I slammed down the phone, sending the Coke can to the hard sidewalk, where it burst open, spraying all over my legs and the opened box of butterflies that had fallen with it.

Inside the box, dirt turned to mud that soaked the once flawless and delicate butterflies. Dyed the fragile and thin paper a murky brown. I sat cross legged on the ground and attempted to pull them apart from one another, ripping the insect right down the middle. As the paper came away in two, I felt something sink just beneath my sternum.

Once I started crying, I just couldn't make myself stop. Not until my head hurt. But I heard a buzz. Right before my eyes each of the butterflies stood, shook off the mud and took flight. Before long there was a large swarm of golden butterflies gently darting in each and every direction. They packed themselves together like a tight fist and then darted outward, forming a swan and then an elephant and then a paper boat.

They settled in the box, now a near translucent white.

"Puddin'! Hurry up!" Erica Jr. waved at me from her position in the swarm of bodies crowded by the race's starting line. All of the fifth graders lined up on the tape that stretched across the street. I could spot Daddy and his cowboy hat right up front. "It's about to start!"

I maneuvered through the mob using my elbows, still holding the box to my chest.

"Hey," Emmanuel grabbed me by the forehead and pulled my head back until he was staring me in my eyes. "You was crying? Why?"

"No, I wasn't." I pulled away and wiped at my face with the back of my hand.

Emmanuel sucked his teeth, "Look at your face, Puddin'."

"How I'm s'posed to do that?"

Then there was Daddy, bent all over next to me, his face inches from mine. "Your cheeks all red. What happened?"

"I already know," Erica Jr. said, grabbing me by the chin. "That ugly-butt girl around the corner. What's her name?"

"Bianca," Emmanuel said.

"That's right. Bug-faced Bianca, didn't know whether to swat her or stomp her!"

Daddy nudged Erica Jr. out of the way, "Your grandma would turn over in her grave if she knew you were letting some ugly little girl get you all bothered. An *ugly* little girl? You're beautiful, look at the man that made you!"

As my lips broke into a smile, the referee fired a shot in the air and the fifth graders took off, some slipping on the asphalt immediately, others tripping over their own feet. Moses sent a look to the left, then the right and took off down the street. Daddy grabbed me up quickly and maneuvered me onto his shoulders. Moses pushed past all of them, first only nosing ahead and then getting a full car length in front of the closest runner.

I balanced myself. Holding the box above Daddy's cowboy hat. I lifted the lid cleanly from the box and one by one, each of the butterflies flew smoothly from the box, riding the gentle breeze that had begun to kick up.

Spa Day at Aunt Mie-Jo's
Laura Doyle Péan

my cousin drops three droplets of oil
on my head
massages my scalp
I sink in

closed eyes   slowed breathing

we hum mourning songs
celebration hymns
welcome the new year
thank the ancestors for independence

she says *it will restore the moisture*
I have always been skeptical
hair product manufacturers
selling us happiness in a bottle
are you convinced your body
doesn't already have
all it needs

skeptical I remain for a while
and she proves me wrong
for days I will gaze into the mirror
stunned by the renewed vigor of my curls
there was still life here

*

adrienne maree brown says pleasure is a measure of freedom. we will be free once everyone has access to the full
range of pleasure they can access. we must do the work
of deconstructing the systems and institutions robbing our
children, our sisters, our trans siblings, and our men of their
joy. we must create opportunities to feel that joy
                — remember how powerful it is —
we must nurture it as if our life depended on it — it does

*

my cousin sits down   orders me
to raise my left foot
the pressure she applies
under my arch
brings the tingle all the way up to my heart
I jump at the newfound sensation
my aunt laughs
everything is connected she says
my cousin repeats the gesture with my right foot
everything is connected repeats my aunt
your grandma knew this
and would rub Vicks all over our feet
during the cold season
to kick out any sickness
my sunshine giggles — their mother
had the same remedy

a warning   or a recipe for liberation
everything is connected and everything that grows and
heals starts from the grassroots level
don't forget to care for your feet
don't forget to care for the land your feet walk on
don't forget about the lands you walk on

Spa Day at Aunt Mie-Jo's

*

Black liberationist, womanist and afrofuturist writer/activist tricia hersey speaks of rest as resistance in a society that has already stolen so much labor from Black folks, communities and nations, and continues to expect us to exhaust ourselves for the benefit of the capitalist economy.

through her work at the nap ministry, she drives people to reimagine what rest can look like and to make it a priority in their lives. in the collective nap spaces she creates, she encourages us to dream more. to love more.

"exhaustion will not save us" she reminds us
"rest will"

*

my sunshine kisses my lips
and my body is submerged by the seashore waves
at sunset
I cry
releasing of all the tension carried
by my great
great grandma
my grandma
my parents
me

I've come to learn not all ties have been
severed with the spirits
they have always been with me
in my bones   my DNA   my dreams
I had just forgotten my way to them

mama didn't want no princess
Shawn Williams

mama didn't want no princess
waiting on her own prince charming
but that's what happens when you raised by a
queen

in mama's closet he did find
all her jewels and pearls divine
and she smiled as he wore her wig as a
crown

mama didn't want no princess
so she told her to always look up
never stumble and walk tall
she didn't want her getting hurt at all

mama loved her lil' princess
that's her baby, her pride and joy
mama knew that one day she'll have a queen
and that's what excited her more

Joy In Her Sole: Remembering My Mother's Shoes
Jeanine DeHoney

This is not a sad story. It is a story about my recollection of my mother's shoes, or rather lack of. But it is still not a sad story. It is a remembering story. And remembering is often in layers. I have to recall some things that may have had faint fragrances of melancholy before I get to the sweetest scent, but it is forthcoming; sometimes when I least expect it, that memory that brought forth joy.

It's similar to how after the rain comes the most beautiful rainbow is painted in the cerulean sky. Or how after death there is always rebirth. That there is a never-ending circle that carries us out of the muddy water blues into abundant joy. That's how I think about my late mother's shoes. So, I hope you bear with me.

There was a time when I couldn't remember her shoes. I couldn't recall whether they were square toed, round toed, pumps, or flats, or whether they had a kitten heel or a wedge to make her taller or whether they were leather or suede or slingback. I didn't remember their colors either, whether they were solely black or brown that complemented any outfit or were gold or silver still in boxes for weddings, or simple black ones for funerals. Even when I dreamt about my mother ... she slipped into those dreams barefoot.

Joy in Her Sole

This troubled me incessantly. For I remembered both my paternal and maternal grandmother's shoes as a little girl, before they grew old and their feet mainly filled slippers given to them for birthdays and Christmas from Sears or JCPenney.

I remember vividly the flat black shoes with thick soles, that laced up, that my paternal grandmother wore to her job as a domestic worker. And I remembered those same lace-up shoes being on my maternal grandmother's feet who was a beautician.

But when it came to my mother, it truly troubled me that I couldn't remember her shoes. We were so close as mother and daughter. I was always underfoot as the youngest daughter. I recollected so many other things about her other possessions in such rich detail. I could name the things she loved and cherished and used or wore the most–all except her shoes. I remembered the flowy, flowered caftans that glided the floor when she walked because they were always too long but she looked queenly in them. I remembered the multiple wigs she wore, the black one she called her Diana Ross wig, and the blond one she called her Marilyn Monroe wig, a red one, a puffy afro one, and even one with braids she called her Cleopatra wig.

And I remembered the black velvet cape she wore with everything when she went out somewhere fancy. I even remembered her collection of Avon lipsticks, and I can close my eyes to this very day and still smell the rose scent of the lotion she rubbed into her brown skin after bathing, and the Chanel No. 5 perfume she dabbed behind her ears and on her wrists, whether she was going out or not. Those flashes of her in my mind will forever flip my frown into a smile. That's the joy I knew so well as a child.

Me not recalling her shoes has often caused me to air-brush a pair of nice-looking well-made shoes on her petite feet whenever I envision her. Even Heaven bound, I did not want my mother to be shoeless. I did not want her to be a woman whose brown toes collected dust and stepped on fragments of debris or for her gait to carry the load of what other people's footsteps left behind, even in my mind's eye.

In the housing development I grew up in, my mother and father's bedroom closet was my favorite place to hide in and play. Under the cloak of their clothes, my father's work clothes, suits, shirts, and pants on one side; my mother's dresses and pant suits on the other side, I'd push her shoes out of the way to settle comfortably on the floor so I could pretend, dream, or write in my black and white note-books. I'd keep their squeaky closet door ajar just a little so I could have enough light to see. And when I was through, I'd gather my belongings, leaving her shoes strewn every which way before closing the closet.

My mother, who loved order in our home, having things in its rightful place, never fussed about her shoes in such disarray. Even today, so many years later, I wonder whether shoes were never important as far as she was concerned. Were they just mere coverings for her feet, nothing more, nothing less? And I wonder if her detached relationship with shoes came about because of her growing up years, when she lost her father at the age of five, before he had time to meld deeply in her spirit.

Shoes wouldn't have mattered much to me either if I'd lost my father at that age, or any age before my heart was imprinted with his soul. I think in the heartbreak and anger and confusion that came from losing a father so young, I would have kicked my shoes off, whether they were old or new, wherever I was standing when I got the news, and shouted at the top of my lungs, "Daddy, Daddy, I want my Daddy!"

My father was always around for me to show off my new pair of shoes when my mother would take my oldest sister and I shoe shopping. Mainly for school, or if we needed a dressy pair, or when I ran the heel of mine down so much from playing outside with my friends and the shoe repair shop couldn't fix it. Going shoe shopping was pure bliss then.

We'd get up early on a Saturday morning and after breakfast, get dressed and take a bus or taxi to either Buster Brown's or Stride Rite in downtown Brooklyn. My favorite part of shoe shopping was watching the salesperson carry a stack of shoe boxes all at one time for the customers. One for me, another for my sister, and at least three other boxes for someone else all on the verge of toppling but somehow, they never did.

Once I tried a pair of shoes on, my mother would press firmly on my big toe to make sure they weren't too tight. Even when I said it wasn't, she'd press on it a few more times, and instruct me to walk around and ask me how they felt, studying my gait like she was an astrologer studying the stars. She'd repeat the same shoe ritual with my sister before letting us carry our new shoes to the register so she could pay for them. And I remember the myriad of styles of shoes we bought then. Black and white saddle shoes, Mary Janes, brown penny loafers, a pair of white and a pair of black patent leather t-straps for church, espadrilles, wedged shoes, and even a sparkly silver pair of shoes for a wedding.

When we got home, I would immediately show my new shoes off to my father. I'd put them on and prance and twirl and wait to hear his deep voice say, "Those are the prettiest shoes ever and you are the prettiest brown girl wearing them." My mother never had that memory to carry along with her like a jazzy melody. I might be wrong because I never broached the subject with her about her father and the void she felt when I became an adult as we sat around her kitchen table talking. But I had heard the stories she herself had gotten secondhand about him and when she told them, I could tell there was an ache there, a gaping hole. And because sometimes I think on a different realm than others, I think because she had no father to show her new shoes off to, or dance on his big shoes with her little shoes like I did with my father so many times until I grew too big, she didn't put much weight into shoes. They didn't matter except as mere coverings for her feet. Nothing more, nothing less.

My mother suffered with chronic heart problems for years and it got progressively worse as she got older. The last time she was admitted to the hospital after several emergencies in which we thought we would lose her; my sister and I knew her life was coming to an end. We began preparing for her not coming home. We went back to her apartment, where we grew up, to talk about our growing up years there and to say our goodbyes to the place where we loved, laughed, cried, and lived life in all of its ebbs and flows.

While my sister cleaned out kitchen cabinets, I went into our mother's bedroom and opened her closet door. It still made a squeaky sound when I opened it. I hadn't looked inside of her closet for such a long time. Once she became ill and was relegated to a hospital bed that we got for her while she was home, we gave most of her clothes and shoes away to a next-door neighbor because she had lost a lot of weight because she'd stopped eating. Her wardrobe consisted of colorful caftans we could easily get her in and out of because she was bedridden. And she mostly wore socks to keep her feet warm so there was no need for shoes.

I picked up a broom and started sweeping the inside of her closet. There was nothing but dust bunnies until I swept towards the back and swept out a pair of black leather pumps with a low heel. And then I smiled and started to remember.

These were the shoes she wore to the supermarket, and I could remember her squeezing fruit and looking for blemishes on it and having my sister and I pick up what else was on her list not caring if we went a little over budget because we always picked up Hostess cupcakes or strawberry shortcake ice cream bars or a bevy of other treats. And I remembered her standing by the deli talking to the person behind the counter like he or she was family while she ordered her favorite Boar's Head ham or turkey, and getting crusty Italian bread, to make us a hero sandwich when we got back home. And she was joyous. Our refrigerator and pantry were full and so were our bellies.

And she wore those shoes to the doctor's office before she got very ill, polishing them with black shoe polish before each appointment to hide any scuffs. And when she got a good doctor's report, she sat in those shoes for a while when she got home, and would call my aunt, her oldest sister, with the news, and she was joyous.

I'm also sure those were the same shoes she wore when she sat in our apartment vestibule with other women on the tenant patrol and when she stood by the door to get petitions signed when we were trying to get certain services in our neighborhood. And when she got those signatures, even from those tenants whose ways made them unapproachable, she was joyous.

She was indeed an activist at heart, and I could see those black low-heeled shoes on her feet, as she had her say about the racism and the wrongs in this world. For that too, that me and my sister and her grandchildren and all children would live in a better world, and that she could play a part in that, would make her heart sing.

For me, shoes chart the seasons in our lives. The shoes we wore as children so easily scuffed by our giggly school playground play, the shoes we wore as teens, ready to spread our wings in the world and soar in our own truth and light and creativity, the shoes we wore as adults, embodying professionalism, and accountability, and then the shoes worn during the latter years of our life; functional, the footsteps of our rhythm hopefully blessed with serenity, our timeclock our own to do as we please.

I've always felt such joy buying shoes and wearing a

myriad of styles. Maybe it was because the women in my life, especially my aunts, loved shoes also. I would watch one of my aunts get dressed for work or on the weekend go out with friends and I would love to watch as she chose a pair of shoes that matched her outfit. Even at church. It wasn't just a hat parade at church that mesmerized me as I sat in the middle pew with my grandmother, it was often a shoe parade as women walked in praising the Lord in all of their Sunday finest. Even then I could tell from the way they walked that there was some joy that radiated from the crowns of their heads to the soles of their feet, especially when the minister was preaching something that got them to shouting in the aisles. Nothing, not even the highest heels, could keep them from praise dancing.

The soles of our shoes not only show the wear and tear from some of the burdens we've carried. But also, the miles we've ambled for celebrations, to dance and laugh till our feet hurt and we've kicked off those darn shoes, like legend Patti LaBelle does at her concerts, because nothing is going to mute our infinite joy. Our shoes cushion not only our feet but our entire soul.

If I was granted one wish today, it would be to go back in time and be a little girl again, going into my mother's closet. I'd take her shoes out pair by pair so I could forever remember them, whether they had a heel or were flat. Whether they were black or brown, suede or leather or sparkly for a wedding. And then I would ask her to try them on and tell them how pretty they were on her feet and how pretty she was and I would take her hand and tell her to twirl around in them, and we would laugh until our bellies ached and joy filled every crevice of our Brooklyn apartment. The apartment she made a home full of memories I will forever cherish. And when she took those shoes off, I would line them up like a set of dominoes, stacking them neatly in the front of her closet like they had been … knowing she still had joy in her soles. She just needed to be reminded it was there even under the hurt of losing her father.

So, you see this is not a sad story. It is a story about my recollection of my mother's shoes, or rather lack of. But it is still not a sad story. It is a remembering story. And remembering is often in layers. I have to recall some things that may have had faint fragrances of melancholy before I get to the sweetest scent, but it is forthcoming, sometimes when I least expect it … that memory that brought forth joy.

What do I feel like I need to say?
Taylor Mckinnon

I got good news today
And I felt it in my chest
And the toils and trials
Of the month the year
Fell through the cracks
Of slipping breaths
And that was that

I turned up my face to the Sun
And the chill of coming winter
And went about my world
With the guilt of romance
And the burden of soiled pots and pans
And the coming need for groceries
Stuck on my shoulders
Like Atlas stood below the earth
And I am smashed by still
Again the joy of breathing Today's breath

Welcome to the Gender Plaground
For mieko ryu
Yeva Johnson

The day I discovered a person could choose
more than one pronoun, the world expanded
in multiple directions and my panda

love found better bamboo forests to call home.
The radical magnet both drawn to
and attracting the feminine in every

person I met, that feminine the nip
to the cat within, romped untamed
but always seen. The dolphin swimmer

carried the queer lesbian who held hands
with the they/them of me on her broad brown
back and we all smiled free in the sun.

When they called me them, I felt so warm
inside that ice cream didn't stand
a chance because I became a femme

with a scoop of neutral on top,
reaffirming my inclination as a child
to choose the gender that, in those

days, could wear dresses AND pants
as the one I liked the best.
When they called me a gay man

Welcome to the Gender Playground

in a lesbian's body, I let it go because
the gay man in me was so turned on by
those scenes in Moonlight, one Black man

reaching, touching, loving another,
even my gorilla philosopher poet,
usually reticent to share, burned

up every time we watched it.
Old as I am, I learned to repurpose
queer, hold the word in my mouth

with pride, let shame dribble
out the sides to the pavement
so that I could become the butch

in blossom or the swirl mixed in
with everything good, the androgynous
of fun expressions. When I took time off

from being the girly girl inside the womon
who could not share her name,
this butterfly post chrysalis, this bug

under the tip of your shoe,
I discovered I'm the Yes And
gender. Look out it's me.

Summer Revolutions
Tiffany Smalls

Allow her to smile, full cheek, full teeth,
suggesting a vacation on the West Coast.
Say yes. Somewhere on a beach,
you'll stack a pile of drift wood to set ablaze.
Sparks flying everywhere,
summer knows that song, plays it at sunset.
Showering stars in the waves, riding like every heartbeat,
young love swelling up on the shore.
Beam bright joy, rival the moon, and her the Earth,
random, ethereal being, you revolve around.
Stunning you, the limbs do not move,
they are frozen March branches, covered
in the last snowfall.
To a degree, you know her league is miles above,
and you might retreat back
to where you think you belong,
but she grabs your hand —
a gentle miracle, pulling you close and her breath
is marshmallows and uncorked wine.
Sip it, dizzy spinning in the sand,
lips moving with that pull between you, closer and closer,
until they collide.

embodiment
Kwame Daniels

i.
we made something for rosacea
a salve
of chickweed and beeswax and olive oil
we sat in a creek
clad in white dress
mud and green soaking the hem
didn't matter that we fell
and fell
and fell again
we were in the creek
our feet touched the rocks
our skin stung with cold
shadowed under leaves
the sun a halo around our hair
the fall is sacred
the love was sacred
the intent of care
brought life to the sitting
the time in a creek
the echo of burbling water
in our ears

ii.
the problem with the bathtub
is that we have to be naked
no matter the kindness of epsom salt

on our pained joints
no matter the earthy smell of white oak bark
and cherry wood perfuming the water
the problem with the bathtub
is that we relax in it
our carefully prepared bath tea
and well-poured salt
easing our pain
until we feel everything else
we see the swell of breasts and belly
we feel our hips settle
the water never goes high enough
that our belly is hidden when we lay back
and our nipples poke from the water
as we roll our shoulders
run our hands over our thighs
feel the push of water between fingers
we are in our skin
we are in our veins
our heartbeat thudding
what else can we do
but hurt?
but fear?
but be?

iii.
it has just rained
my feet squelch on the ground beneath the grass
part of Maryland used to be swampland
the land remembers
blades of grass sharp and slick
brush wet against our ankle

embodiment

last night
we poured hot water
over calendula petals
this morning
we wet our hands with the tea
rubbed it on our face
to greet the sun with our skin smooth

we sink to our knees
jeans grow wet
and we let the wind touch us
and the light caress us

we think
there are better days to come

See the Skinny Lady by the Fire Hydrant
Regina Jamison

I know enough to get her shirt off
unbutton her jeans
whisper something in her ear

in the basement
a candle lit
we bend space together
do it in the kitchen while water boils
her long hair covering my face
our bodies inverted
structures measured beyond shadow
beyond the equation of limbs

this is not a giant leap
more like compassion
or a side step between

(Found in "V" poem by Matthew Dickman)

edaphoecotropism
Ashia Ajani

at the dawn, i am abuzz with yearning
i dust the pollen from my legs
                eager to be enveloped once again
in your precious nectar
the mirror reflects what i am
while i sculpt myself into who i could be
a tree can grow around an object, engulfing
hard metal in its wooden embrace
so i let desire wrap its tall arms around me
         and tether my eager appendages
to its ever-expanding anatomy

before sun graces my window, lust awakens me
though these two needs fill different hankering
               both make all life possible, and
if i am granted a half-hour glimpse of you at break
i feel the tree tightening its green grip
for you i brushed myself into a dazzling creek
              rusting an old oil can into memory
simply for a glimpse of your hand in an indirectly lit
hallway
like a dazzling touch-me-not, skeptical of any strange
caress but still unfurls its arms towards
             the warmth of a guiding star

every morning was my Creation story
i lined my mouth a glossy scarlet
        erupting firecracker orange honeysuckle

from a repatriated fence
sweetness dripping with every pursed lip, just for you
i showed you what the body can do
when it is willing
      knocking seasons from your limbs
restoring you brilliant, evergreen

one day they will carve into you, my love
      as they do most brown things that have found
a way to weather the worst impositions placed on
rooted territory
      someone will take an ax to this gentle body
challenge you to split at the core
maybe the steel will chip at the miracle of our figures
intertwined – maybe my tough spine will spill
      enough sap to dull whatever blade
tries to slice through our verdant haven
and maybe, just maybe that won't be enough

for now embrace me as I grasp at your flavor
come lay the sparkle of your starlit smile
against my paintbrush tongue
           and watch how a concrete jungle springs
a new well of color

bait II master
Whitney French

"Pleasure evokes change more than shame"
— adrienne maree brown

you are not who you desire
you are not who you eat
slide into a bathtub
to melt shame   melt fear

get out of the way
of your own lust &
be aroused by your own
breathless gasp

lavish
in warmth
lavish
     longer

now squeeze time
out of orgasm & connect
to the cosmos
pooling between your legs

you are more
than you desire
you transform
into what is required of

   — the body knows no consequences tonight:

go ahead, slide into a passion so
long deserved & bellow
from glistened lips
yes! reshape ecstasy

to outmatch your politic
   until it engulfs you.

Two Alone in Public
Jasminum McMullen

I want to hold down the beach sands with you
describe the sounds waves make
until daybreak
skinny dip in the depth of your stare
soak up the silence underneath the moonlight
and eavesdrop on the conversation between our hearts

stars beat in the sky for us
the 808 thump of it summons a flirtatious wind,
a gentle kiss through your hair sprouts wings
flies into the stick of your lip gloss and hangs there
like broken cobwebs anchoring the top of a door frame
interrupting the thought train advancing you tunnel
your mouth with intimate requests
pull up to my drive-thru speak-ear

I tell you, I can serve it fast, but you'll have to eat slow
a gasp fills the space between your giggled response to
provoking the slick talk in me

siren smile lust
spread and rise to the surface of my skin
and I glow brighter than the moon
because of you and hard as stone
where it counts

You are dynamite fine with a lit fuse
I'm weak like rotted wood fences

when I'm near you
I'm weak like Maxwell House Sanka
with an ice cube

I am under your spell like a slip of paper
beneath a book of black magic
holding the details; mix well
in your heated cauldron

and even though I caused the fire
know that I am not fire retardant
so when the flame roars, I'm consumed by it

ashes to ashes
I don't mind it
as long as we are two alone
in public touching in private

My Lisa Bonet Obsession
Regina Jamison

Her eyes haunt me like small towns gone belly up
Louisiana lashes dark and heavy as old photographs
voice smooth as Delta Blues then shredded / crumbled

> her arms be Banyans rooted in a down dog position
> pressed into yoga mats instead of my arms which
> are just as soft just as sturdy with my back against
> the floor I see the size of her breasts matches
> the circumference of my open mouth, titties dangling

I say: Bonet … girl, whatcha doin' in this place, this time,
spirits made slits of your eyes; I saw them ride you
so many years ago, turned you tissue paper
thin, I watched you beside me then, the tips of my hair
turned blonde by the California sun, my skin blazed
but yours looked so cool your arms covered in soft
down, pale as a grasshopper's wings,

> plantain or was it
> pineapple in your frail hands, words alone could
> break you, so I stayed silent, but I longed to touch
> your locks
> so heavy against your hips, how they reached for
> your toes
> like strangle trees capture / encase
> like bougainvillea vines
> attach their flowers to our world

all about love
Taylor King

you
and
i
a union that is
soul fated
divinely orchestrated

a love that is
reminiscent of the unions before us that got it right
one that makes the pain from our prior lovers feel worth it
one that makes generational traumas fall at our feet

i can't tell you how long this will last
but sometimes when i look at you
(especially in your element)
i can see years at a time
but it almost seems impolite
to make this union man-made
through the concept of time
so i take it a day at a time
to show spirit i'm in the moment
and i take away my sense of control
with the need to know how long i have you to myself
as if i was God enough to have a hand in that

If Beale Street Could Talk
Shawn Williams

If Beale Street could talk, what would he say?
He took me down to the jazz club
For our first date
Imagine
Two lil' Black boys
Snapping
Clapping
Tapping
Away to the sweet tunes of the Blues
As the men crooned and trumpets boomed
I was swoon
He took me by the arm and we danced
Right then and there
And while we looked blue underneath that moonlight
We was far from it
What a story to tell as he walked me
Arm in arm towards the subway station
While the last notes of that sweet
Melody played into that warm
June night
If Beale Street could talk, what would he say?

Mirror of Life
Patrick Sylvain

In the undulating mirror
of life, your face flows
in a river. I reach to touch
the smooth slope of your cheeks,
waves thrust away my hand
as time seizes your youth.

I wanted to dive after you,
but a mallard duck dips
its yellow bill into the river
disturbing my sight. I close
my eyes, savoring the screen
of a quotidian picture;
you, alluringly dancing.

Black curly hair swooshing
to your face as your undulating body
responds to Beyoncé's "Love on Top."
I swim to your smile, tasting
your aromatic sweat. The duck
splashes water as it flaps its wings.
I'm back on land, still holding on
to a memory that blushes at us.

To: Whom It May Concern
RE: Black Joy
Regina YC Garcia

Upon the purchase of a Black History Month t-shirt,
one that almost *shut me down* in my local Target,
chanting at me from the racks
Radiate Black Joy
I determined that it was my time to shine, radiate, unwind
ALL of my joy! Yet,

as I lay the shirt across my bed, face
set on 'grateful' for my find, my ancestors moved
from my belly, up into my opened ears, and I heard their
whispers, words not relegated to the intentional, traditional
observations of Black History. I stood, picked up the shirt,
slid it over my head, and was divinely compelled to consider, to list the layers, for myself and others, of what it means
to radiate *Black* joy. For if we are honest, this *Black* joy, as
a construct, is shaped by the misshapen circumstances of
history, for indeed *Black* joy is

what is birthed between bouts of *Black* pain
        It is molded to sustain
        It is compelled to keep moving
        through one degree of uncertainty to the next
It is the production of delicacies
        from disposable waste
It is the retention of The Spirit
        that has been carried in ancestors
        from generation to generation

hidden and released in clearings
introduced through uttered prayers and praise, and
It emerges in various forms
sometimes like tears
sometimes like immovability
It can even hide under other feelings
mask in mysteries,
cloak in glances, in ways of speaking
laugh behind closed eyes and lips
While yet another layer of joy plants the seeds
of the knowledge
that there are golden pieces of *Black* gifting,
of *Black* strength, even of *Black*
prophecy that cannot be removed from
Black existence.
That is that *Black* joy-
knowing that even in derision, there is provision
in this joy that secrets us
and the gifts that save us
This joy that reminds us that
trouble don't last always
weeping endures for a night
joy comes in the morning light

And at times, good times, *Black* joy requires *Black*
bodies to throw back their heads and
laugh loudly and move freely
play Spades
The Dozens
dance
love
create
create
create
share

To: Whom It May Concern

care
Save the whole world

The children know that there is love
Just there
In *Black* joy
And for ALL who may be concerned
Know *this-*
While this joy is juxtaposed to pain
the glory is that it can
Emerge
again, and again
Black Joy
Shine
Radiate
Refine
Create
More and more
Great God! Black joy!
You tell anyone else who wants to know
Just tell them to go on and
know that there is more in store
from this brilliant, unbelievably resilient
Black
Joy

Indigo Road
Keisha-Gaye Anderson

She descends with laughter every time,
this ancestor
Because, how can you ever lose what you are,
girl?

We walk the indigo road, she says
is so chatty,
the mambo
needs a sip of cool water

She say we
called Fula
called Yoruba
called Old Kingdom
but be even older than all that wahala

And time demands
I come into my mother's house
the living ocean

My mamas be
women stepping out of the night sky
to teach
to shape
to spin the world into
balance
in their centers
dissolve the blindness of men

Indigo Road

with patient blue hands
healing hands
the color that could only come from
the volcanic fire
of the Great Mother

And I am them, too
they have never let me go,
she wants me to know
says we are still working
for the new time
the new day
that requires new language
to purge the thickness of electric living
information quicksand
dull drone of destruction
stacked in steel and cinder
over our graves

I will stay on the path,
mother

Thank you.

Porkchops
Esperanza Cintrón

Mama sat
knees and feet tight
at the edge of my bed
a narrow bunk
in a dorm room
freshman year
The plate on her lap
was wrapped in
snug tucked foil
Her driver, an old man
a neighbor from up the block
sat near the desk
in the only chair
She just wanted to see,
to let me feel her pride
because the words
would never be said
But I could smell
the crisp fried chops
creamy potatoes and sweet peas
a testament to her skill
and my favorites

We come up
Elizabeth Mudenyo

There is ginger beer, beer beer, red wine, white wine,
brown liquor, cold water, sweat flows, hips wind,
deep sighs, gut groans, loud mouths, belly laughs,
gapped tooth, sweet tooths, shy eyes, hot takes,
good food barbecued jerked boiled pan fried
stewed & simmered

your tongue is out, your chest is out, arms out,
fros out, heads wrapped, smells like shea like
cocoa like ganja like coconut oil like not a dry
elbow in the house all our lips are plump
lyric shinin to and fro

not a head the same
& everyone knows we braid together
we remember your pronouns your sun sign
where you grew up what you adopt

everyone knows the vibe
& all the ancestors come thru
we count from now & your spirit never broke
we get high we get still & finally

see who blinks first, cracks a smile,
buckles without saying
How I've missed you

Pilot
Akua Lezli Hope

My copilot says nothing of my cockpit juju
after hundreds of hours and tens of thousands of miles
through clouds
our successful earth circling transport assures him

I believe we ask for each other, an easy team,
yet one I must manage more than I prefer
I like a bit of banter and someone who knows
when silence lends speed to adjustments
as we clamber above dwindling skyscrapers
to kiss blue sky

I like telling folks where to look and what's approaching
I shape it—not too chatty, not too crisp,
have them feel guided and not directed
put my spin on this American construct, show and tell
> *we'll have to circle New York City*
> *path of our arrival today*
> *will take us over Yankee Stadium*
> *and past the Statue of Liberty and*
> *Ellis Island on the left*

won't say, where all four grandparents landed
won't say, over Harlem where they lived within 4 blocks of
each other
will remember they saw Bessie Coleman barnstorming
told me: first black, first woman to get her pilot's license,
before Amelia

Pilot

(though sure, *we* flew without vehicles)
Bessie sharecropped, laundered, then hairdressed to
earn money,
studying, then studying French in Chicago, to study flying
in France
just after the first World War
woman with wings with wings with wings
my patron saint, sharp in the aviatrix outfit she
commissioned,
leather jacketed, helmeted, a fox of an ace

and Uhura, not real, but necessary pretending
on a cardboard set to be a fly sister in space,
inspiring Dr. Mae J. to astronautical pioneering

my triumvir, and gold wing charm from my parents,
pouched, cosseted and near in my command center,
in my organ field of lights and switches
before the clear treble strength windshield above the nose
where sometimes I will hear the song of nothing in the
dim hum,
of earth and all

And they wink out and on again
a screaming blink tells me power is gone
chalk and gasoline in my mouth,
my stomach both punch and the fist
lightning flash. iron scent. polycarbon funk. then open palm
deep breathe. Check the gear.

copilot white as a cloud. making calls
ghosting already
forestalling a bleak inevitable
                when inertia is your friend

when up is up so stay up
when go is go so stay going
and all you know is not enough
so use your unknowing
through air unpowered,
too heavy for thermals just
so high, so high so high up in the sky
how grave mass becomes
impetus of   *moving, moving on*
calculated trajectories, inertia
moving my metal body
what skill to bring to bear
after years and years and tears
of calculating angles patterns pasts

> *if I had the wings of a dove*
> *if I had the wings of a dove*
> *I would fly away home, fly away home*

grandmother's singing comes to me
o Mama! and all my everloving Gone,
sing me, guide me, lead me on
drop me in the water

did Tubman, ground bound,
guiding hundreds to freedom's safety
ever lose a passenger? movering movering

Nor will I.
lives nested in fragile shells
we're gonna land with eggs unbroken
my gear extends. my metal wings feather
blue appears to greet me
I'm piloting this plane to glory

Pilot

Bessie Coleman 1892-1926 first African American and first woman to be awarded a pilot's license—she received hers two years before Amelia Earhart.

Dr. Mae Jemison, the first African American female astronaut.

Uhura, the communications officer of the starship Enterprise, a character portrayed by actor **Nichelle Nichols,** who said the Reverend Dr. Martin Luther King, Jr. urged her to remain with the *Star Trek* series when she considered leaving.

Birth
Audrey Williams

…listening with your heart
strong bonds nourishing
wonder, joy, happiness abounds
tiny feet, little hands, sweet smiles
perfection captured in the details
angels captured in the eyes

On the Eighth Day
Àjokẹ́ Bódúndé

Guests flood in,
shoes gather like debris on your doormat:
                    a rainbow   of   kitten heels,
slacking   slings,
palm slippers   posing   in   new sheen.
Men in fila tuck talking drums
underneath armpits,
each thud   a naming.
Inside-elders-are-shelved-beside-each-other-bookmarked-
by-walking-sticks.
They chew loudly on kola-nut.
Here, there are gifts you do not open alone.
The baby is wrapped in embroidered lace ivory,
cooing while she sleeps.
In the fullness of her lips,
spread   of   her   nose,
she resembles her father.
The~squeeze~of~her~coils~matches~yours.
          IS SHE GOING TO GET DARKER,
          LIKE US?
Rave little girls you've helped into dresses.
You nod your head,
watch the black in their eyes beam.

I Will Be Loud
Akua Lezli Hope

Preach what soul-hampering things you may
thin-lipped, ice-veined naysayers
I will never refuse joy, even if it may annoy
I will always be proud and laugh out loud
I will never deride delight
for all the sparks it unerringly ignites
whose lit fuel creates much needed warmth and light
and helps us survive monster-riddled nights
and endure blood-spattered, pandemic days

The Black Beatitudes (For Black Women)
Sienna L.M.

And seeing the different shades from afar, she came closer to witness them and said:

"*Blessed* is the Black woman, brown in the body: for the benefits of melanin are hers.

Blessed is the Black woman who is labeled strong when she is weak: for it is in her human nature to be both.

Blessed is the Black woman's silent tears: for they shall nurture her earth.

Blessed is the Black woman who hungers and thirsts after healing: for she shall make her own way if there is no path.

Blessed is the Black woman who is melanin-full: for she shall obtain sunlight.

Blessed is the Black woman's tone—of voice and skin—for they both have been touched by Me.

Blessed are the Black mothers: for they were and are the bearers of Light's children.

Blessed is the Black woman who is discriminated against for healing's sake: for trauma ends with her.

Blessed are you, Black woman, when the world and even your own kind, are unkind to you—stigmatize you, oppress you, and falsely teach you to hate yourself.

Rejoice and let your heart become—*Black girl lips*—plump with joy when other Black women create spaces for celebrating your happiness."

Subway Therapist; Finding Joy in Subterranean New York
Marlee Miller

It was Mischief Night in New York City and I made my way towards the uptown F train platform at the Delancey-Essex stop. Beneath my feet were grimy tiles, each one like a kitchen-sponge caked with a century's worth of filth and germs. The platform was crowded and I narrowly missed stepping in a long stream of bright red liquid leaking from a to-go cup. The F train is usually delayed; the station brimmed with impatient New Yorkers.

Through the hustle and bustle, I could hear percussion sounds and music. I turned towards the center of the platform where I saw people standing in a semi-circle around a tap dancer.

I was transfixed.

It had been just six days since I finished a week-long stay in a Mount Sinai Hospital psychiatric ward on the Lower East Side. My stay there started with the unassailable belief that I wanted to end my life.

But now, on the subway platform, I felt life breathed into me as I watched the tap dancer. He was so alert and dedicated to *his* living that he was breathing life into everything around him. Each breath a clap of metal making swift contact with a three by one-foot wooden board beneath him. His stamina was as impressive as his skill. Each fall of his ball, toe, or heel felt deliberate despite the fact that he was improvising with the different beats and tempos blaring from the speaker next to him.

The dancer stood about 5'8" and he had a kind and tender smile framed inside a goatee. Sweat-glistened on obsidian skin and, occasionally, it would take flight from his neatly shaped hi-top fade.

The mix of spectacle and precision enthralled me. The tap dancer performed an infinite number of combinations of beats and rhythms with his feet and he did it as fast as humanly possible. The minute I found myself lulled by one rhythm, he switched to another combination. At the same time, he made various shapes with different parts of his body. One second, his figure was as small as possible; the next, he was large and imposing.

One second his chiseled arms stretched in a straight angle; the next, his elbows bent inward and he hunched forward. He created a half-circle from the chest up and tapped out a pattern with the apex of his shoe. His legs rapidly separated at an obtuse angle before coming in closer together. Then his arms flew out to the side again like the wings of an exhilarated Sandhill Crane performing a courtship dance.

I could see how mindful of a listener the dancer was. His feet rose and fell in a way that paired perfectly with the beats of the music.

The tap dancer was a physical manifestation of Black joy, and not just because he was smiling through his dance.

I had spent the last week struggling to reacclimate and renovate myself. This moment with the dancer proved critical. I felt my brain release a substantial exhale it had been holding in for a month.

For once my mind wasn't frantic. For once it was still. The fast steps of a dancer calmed me. His whole body was an instrument.

I looked around at others who had gathered to watch as if to ask them with my eyes: "Are you *seeing* this?"

Two Black girls standing on the other side of the tap dancer answered my unspoken question. They were young, maybe five or six. One was wearing a pastel pink tutu that matched the beads in her cornrow braids. The other, a little younger, shorter, wore a black and purple witch costume. Both were holding plastic jack-o-lantern buckets, perhaps on their way to go trick-or-treating. They were both enraptured, staring at the dancer.

At one point, an adult woman – maybe their mother – who stood behind them, handed each of the girls a couple of dollars. They both ran giddily towards the box in front of the dancer and paused before the taller girl dropped the cash in the box and shyly looked up at the dancer. He grinned gingerly, still in mid-dance.

I fought my tears and half-laughed at myself for being so sentimental. But something happened that day. The tap dancer had awakened something inside me. I felt alive in a way that I hadn't felt in a long time.

I suspect I am not alone in what I felt on that subway platform. Therapists have long studied what happens in our brains when we witness someone else's narrative.

*

Subway Therapist

I was curious about my brain's reaction to seeing the dancer's performance. I tracked down two professionals who enthusiastically agreed to answer some of my questions.

Dr. Kristin Long, a psychoanalyst and Creative Arts therapist, told me about the role of mirror neurons and bilateral stimulation. Saying someone's smile is contagious is not just a cliché. Mirror neurons are a class of neurons that discharge in the same way both when an individual performs a particular action, as well as when they observe another person performing the same action. By witnessing the dancer's narrative of joy, my brain was able to release its own dopamine or "pleasure chemical."

Bilateral stimulation, often used in EMDR therapy (eye movement desensitization and reprocessing), is using something you can see, hear, or feel and when crossing the body in a rhythmic pattern, Long said, that kind of stimulation has been known to decrease anxiety levels and cause relaxation, as well as increased attention flexibility. Meaning your thoughts become less 'stuck' on whatever was bothering you. And dancing, especially tap dancing, is one of the most effective forms of bilateral stimulation, Long said.

Mr. Callum Fedele, who works at the same practice as Long, is working towards becoming a fully-licensed Creative Arts Therapist. He pointed out that self-regulation or regulating our emotions isn't often something that's taught.

As a Black woman diagnosed with Bipolar II, I'm deeply familiar with the challenges that come with not knowing how to control my emotions.

"I wonder if there was an element of you regulating

how you were feeling through using that moment as a pro-jective by identifying with, feeling the vibrations from, the energy coming off of that person," Callum told me. "You know, the full somatic experience of that moment."

*

The dancer had his Instagram handle printed on a sign next to him while he performed. I followed him immediate-ly and DM'd him a couple days later to see if he'd be open to chatting with me. His name is Ja'Bowen Dixon. He is a multidisciplinary artist who was born and raised on the west side of Chicago in North Lawndale. Ja'Bowen describes the long block he grew up on as a tight-knit community of folks who were friendly and communicative.

Not only is Ja'Bowen a professional tap dancer, but he's also an actor, writer, rapper, and singer, and is currently working on trying to blend the different art forms he prac-tices. He has been surrounded by tap dancing his whole life and considers his older brother, Bril Barrett, a catalyst for his own dancing career. Bril was six when he started tap dancing through a program called The Better Boys Founda-tion, at a neighborhood youth center. Ja'Bowen was also six when he took his first tap lesson with Bril.

He tells me he moved to Brooklyn in January 2020 with his partner, Nicole, after she was cast in the musical "Six" on Broadway. After everything shut down about three months later, the couple ended up moving back to Illinois for almost a year due to tight funds. When things started to open up again, they moved back to New York and settled in

Subway Therapist

Brooklyn's Bedford–Stuyvesant neighborhood. Ja'Bowen picked up a teaching job at Brooklyn Center for the Arts.

He decided he would make extra money on the side and get to know the city by performing improvised tap dances in subterranean New York. The subway system can be chaotic but Ja'Bowen quickly realized that it could also be a rather intimate setting. He could perform for diverse crowds of people from all walks of life. And he could do so in one of the most familiar and densely populated parts of the city. He felt as though it also proved to be a good way to bring art and performance to those who may not always have access to it.

"I want that to be at the base of a lot of what I do," Ja'Bowen shares one autumn day over a coffee. "I want to keep this art accessible to those it might otherwise not be, particularly within the Black community."

Sure, he performs for the throngs of tourists in stations like Time Square; that's when he wants to make money. But he also frequents largely Black Brooklyn neighborhoods "to bring the art to people who aren't always offered the opportunity to be more attuned with their creative side."

Ja'Bowen once formally taught tap dancing classes for kids in Chicago. I think about the two little Black girls who were watching him perform at Delancey-Essex. I also think about how in so many ways, our society makes prioritizing creative expression a luxury only some can afford.

But dance is so inherently a part of Black culture. It is ancestral.

Dr. Long, a white therapist, pointed to research that says one of the many reasons talk therapy is so common in

Western white culture is because ritualistic movement, music, and dance have in many ways been devalued or eliminated. By using dance and movement as a modality for communication, Black folks are preserving their roots and decolonizing language.

From the tribal dances of our African ancestry – which are still thriving to this day – to Frankie Manning's Lindy Hop and Cab Calloway's Jitterbug. Ja'Bowen mentions names from the world of tap dancing who inspire him; The Nicholas Brothers, Gregory Hinds, and Jimmy Slide. Dance and music as communication, celebration, and acts of resistance have been there even during the most horrid parts of our history. Despite everything, we still manage to move with joy.

*

"You're sharing your soul through creative expression, and I think that resonates with people," he says. "People feel very comfortable coming up to me afterwards and telling me their life story. I'm almost like a subway therapist."

I laugh, absolutely delighted by the term "subway therapist." But, as I chew on the term for a moment, I realize that it sounds like a heavy profession. And Ja'Bowen did mention that he is careful not to take on other people's woes as his own.

He recounts a story about a man who told him he had just gotten out of jail and was trying to turn his life around. I feel a little sheepish remembering how I told Ja'Bowen about my time in the psych ward. On cue, as though he could read my thoughts, he says, "At the end of the day, I do appreciate that people feel comfortable with me. It means the most to me when I get that one-on-one connection with someone who wants to share themself as well."

I've seen Ja'Bowen perform in the subway three times and he never falters in his meditative joy. It's like he speeds up time. Usually, when the F train is 15 to 20 minutes away, the rushed New Yorker inside me moans and groans and the minutes pass by at a glacial pace. But when Ja'Bowen is performing on the platform, time goes too fast. The train comes and I almost feel robbed of something. I'm left wanting more.

The space Ja'Bowen suggested we meet is a designated workspace with a built-in cafe in Williamsburg, Brooklyn. People are able to rent enclosed offices for an hour or two while they work. The two of us are sitting in a more open lounge-style area. We're surrounded by people seated at nearby tables who are diligently typing away with their earbuds in.

At first I was worried the space would be too distracting for us to have a real conversation. But similar to the experience of watching Ja'Bowen dance, I am completely immersed in our discussion.

Ja'Bowen looks up towards the ceiling as if carefully considering how to articulate his next thought. He leans forward in his chair and touches the surface of the circular table between us with his right index finger. "Everyone has a purpose," he says while tapping the table. The tip of his finger rises up and down, emphasizing the cadence of each word. "We may not be aware of or attuned with that purpose and we might be searching for it."

I try not to laugh. Not because what he's saying is funny but because it feels like the universe is poking fun at me and also providing some eerily specific divine intervention. I say this because day four in the psych ward was the first time I actually participated verbally in one of the daily scheduled support groups. It was the first day I wasn't too pissed at my situation to speak.

An 18-year-old woman who sat across from me in matching sky-blue scrubs and gray grippy socks responded to a question posed by the group facilitator: "Where in your life do you feel connected? Where do you feel a disconnect?"

The young woman responded by saying she felt disconnected from a purpose. She was excited for her freshman year of college in New York City and expected it to be awesome, but now she was failing all her classes and landed herself in the psych ward. She almost dismissed herself as she was speaking.

"I know I'm only 18," she said. "I'm young and I have time to figure it out, but I don't know."

As she trailed off, I tried to affirm her. In my head I thought, *Girl, I'm 29, and I'm in the same boat*. I hadn't realized until she verbalized her disconnect that I felt the same exact way.

I let the thought pass and hone my thoughts on Ja'Bowen.

"The artistry," he says, referring to primarily his tap dancing, but also the other mediums and creative outlets he utilizes, "is just a conduit for me to share the energy of that purpose that I believe I have."

Ja'Bowen's main goal is to spread positivity. And this seemed almost obvious to me the first time I saw him dance.

Custodians were sweeping around us and packing up displays in the work space where we conversed. We got up to leave and Ja'Bowen said he would invite me over to his house one day soon.

"I hope you know we're friends now," he says.

*

I have thought a lot about Ja'Bowen's subway performances. At first, I thought I found it transformative because it acted as an antidote or maybe a disruption of the depressing nature of the mundane.

But it was so much more than that.

Often, when we tell Black stories, we center our survival or how we mitigate extreme pain and oppression. And yes, centering Black joy is a form of survival. But what does it look like to manifest our exultation and share it with others so that they can see it's possible, even when they don't feel it?

Sometimes we need a reminder. My reminder came in the form of Ja'Bowen and the tap of his shoes.

Music's Melody
Audrey Williams

Music hangs on a breeze
that flows waif-like
softly, caressing;

you move fluently
your giftedness & joy
lightly touches as you flex
and withdraw again;

the melody whispers,
the body expands,
causing swells and ripples
in vibrational realms.

Feast Day, Celebration of the 1863 Emancipation Proclamation
doris diosa davenport

as i prepared a feast for my 3 GA sistahs & me
some Kinsperson whom i love, maybe not enough,
wants more attention, specifically so
compelled me back to the store scrounging
the *smoked meat* section for
ham hocks.   Possessed, i, a pacifist vegetarian,
was about to bash a small Mexican child in the head,
or elbow the elderly fragile ytfemale, to reach that
last package, so glad as they made
other odious choices leaving me (whew!)
with the prized last package

but to my *conscious* knowledge i have
never prepared this meal
maybe past lifetimes – suppressed, forgotten, denied
yet here they bubble in my cauldron-pot
covered in alchemical hot water, collards & onions;
cayenne, black pepper & salt – whatever else i got,
to cover that smell to season that taste. With this prayer –

Dear Benign Deceased Ancestors,
Foremamas and Male-creators too
let me praise you in all i do – serve your memory every day
but this is it with the ham hocks okay? No more.

(Enjoy)

Holding the Sun
Taylor King

to have the honor to experience
a love greater than all the loves i have known
just a taste will suffice
when i sit back and think about the many times
i was in love
or so i thought
this has to be the most true
an unconditional love
without a qualification
without an expectation
without a justification
just me and you
you, half of me
me, all of you

for nine months i held the sun
and now i walk alongside it
i need sum florida wata
to cleanse my hands
for holding you
and to cleanse my feet
and walk next to you
light some sage
to even think of you
baby
it's only pure air that my
"i love you's"

Holding the Sun

cascade in
before they dance in your ear

i was chose
despite of
my flaws
and short comings
insecurities
traumas
ego

*to my sunshine or sonshine:
my gift. i have had the privilege to be a vessel for
your transformation into the physical realm. and i
am honored.

Continuous Spring
For Blue Rabbit

Patrick Sylvain

You winged into my life like a radiant butterfly
Lodging spring in my spine, I've flowered ever since.

Although we have not had a chance to watch
The lifting of morning dew into murmur, we've eased

Into fall's starlights without distancing our orbit.
Our time is the peaceful construction of our web.

From fanning summer moments to long and crisp winter
Nights, we've rumpled the sheets creating our own fervor.

We are each other's fire and despite our tumultuous pasts
We've steadied the lines deciding to enduringly hang
our hearts

On our spring. Content with our continuous blossoming
We've disavowed our thorny gardeners and abluted
our soil.

We are almost ready to plant African Violets and soon
We'll watch them develop and oscillate in the
summer wind.

Elated, you winged into my life like a radiant butterfly
Ushering in triumphant and incessant laughter.

At Last
Elvis Alves

Before my kids came along,
graduation from college was
a moment of delight. But
that was an accomplishment
or something akin to it.

I tell my wife that I had a front row
seat to witness doctors pull life
from her body. A moment of
delight that happened twice.

Want to know the first thing that
 I did in the moment? I counted
 the toes of the babies.

In the hush of it all, and counting of
toes, was praise for gratitude felt
at last.

Holding a Moment
Keisha-Gaye Anderson

I would like to hold this day
suspend it forever,
freeze the ever-moving river that pulls
us through doorways of experience
and hard resets
of the real
as we see it
to watch a silly movie
with my daughter
her fuzzy twisted head
of hair in my lap
"Rub my head, mom…"
and listen to my son
the bass voice
still sounding like a boy to me
as he talks of philosophy
and, "Mom, did you know…?"
as I rediscover what is new to them
but old to everyone with silver streaks like mine
and we just smile
silent
don't spoil the surprise
the unfolding of living
for them
This perfect moment
on a faded couch
with take-out food
a frisky cat

Holding a Moment

and their father
so reserved
smiling when he thinks we aren't looking
pretending he is not transformed back into a teen
when naming all the flags of the world in a trivia game
with his teen son
We bop to the sound of our girl
playing one of her new guitar songs
And I want to loop that melody
I want to hold this fullness
this contentment
this joy of
simple togetherness
forever
like a seed in a vault
that can end a hunger
which I know will inevitably reach my door
But not today

Dirty, Warped, & Cracked
Stephanie Andrea Allen

What if the lens through which you came to know yourself
was dirty, warped, and cracked?
  Do you scrape off the sick with a scalpel
    Or splash it with bleach, leaving sorrowed streaks?
  Do you shatter the glass with the hammer of your pain?
    Or seal the cracks with salve, conjured from your tears?
  Do you sand the warp with the terror of your torment
    Or buff them smooth, with the scour of your rage?

What if the lens through which you came to know yourself
was only an illusion?
  And you could alter its image with your will
  And you were cleansed in the canals of love and affection
  And your heart was nourished with the promise of
  infinite dreams
  And your wounds were sutured with the thread of hope
  And your scars were soothed with shea until they ceased
  to exist

And you were flying among the stars?

Mz. Myjoy's Joyful Interview
S. Renée Bess

Note to the reader: If you ask writers how they invent fictional characters, more than a few will say they've met certain characters in their books whose presence continues to exist well after a book has been written. Mz. Myjoy Henderson is one such character. She first introduced herself to me when I searched for someone who would understand and help sustain Roberta Baker in *The Rules*. Since then, she's visited me numerous times. Sometimes she pops up silently as if to remind me that she's still around. Other times, she cannot quiet or still her wisdom and wit. All of the time she encourages me to listen and watch as people reveal themselves, either by design or accident. You cannot conceal your true self from Mz. Myjoy.

The second I arrived at the town park, I noticed the young woman waiting for me wasn't wearing a mask to protect herself and anybody else from getting Covid. I patted my pants' pocket where I'd stuffed mine, pulled it out and put it on. True, we were outside, but I wasn't taking any chances. Who knew where this young woman had been and with whom?

She was busy setting up her equipment and didn't seem to see me. In one hand she held a flat, silver rectangle the size of a thin book, an "i" something or other. A fancy cell phone, which was too big to make much sense, peeked above her shirt pocket, and a small camera swung from side to side near her hip. The tiny thing clung to one end of a cord. The other end of the cord was clipped to the woman's worn canvas belt.

I wondered if that camera's miniscule lens would fit all of me within its borders.

I've always been weight conscious, especially when I was younger. When words like "chubby, robust, and fatso" pierced my skin and made me feel that was all I was, nothing more. Now I know the worth of every pound on my body and every hair that's slowly turned gray. I can focus on more important things. Like this interview for example.

The park was really the town square. I liked referring to it as a park because it was more than a patch of grass with wood benches spaced at its perimeter. Here and there were shrub beds filled with witch hazel, red buckeye, and camellias. A clutch of longleaf pines competed with each other for the title of "tallest." My favorite tree was the old osage orange tree. It's double-branched trunk and wide leaf canopy were pure royalty. I named that tree, "The Great I Am."

So, it was fitting that the interview would take place in the middle of the park, under the shade of that particular tree, and somewhat away from the noise of any cars and trucks passing by. The damp warmth from the mid-morning sun was simply a hint of the heat we'd feel by noon, not to mention later on in the day.

I moved closer to the young woman and pointed at a tall chair, "Good afternoon. Is this where you want me to sit?"

"Oh, hello," she said. "Yes, please sit down. My name is Sandy, by the way."

"Nice to meet you, Sandy."

I approached the chair and hoped Sandy didn't read my slow movements as my reluctance to sit where she wanted me to. I got closer to the seat and took a measure of it. Pulling in a deep breath, I pushed the toes of my left foot firmly against the ground and hoisted myself, right side first, onto the stool. Of all the kinds of chairs there are in the world, stools were my least favorite. I'd never liked them, probably because of my height, or lack of it. But I had to confess that this particular stool wasn't bad. Its smooth, weathered leather seat accepted the shape of my hips as if it had known them for a lifetime.

"Are you ready to begin, Ms. Henderson?" the young woman asked.

"Sure."

I watched her tap a series of buttons on her phone and that "i-something-or-other."

"Your first name is quite unusual. I've never known anyone named Myjoy."

"A lot of people have told me that, Ms. … what's your name again?"

"It's Sandy."

"Well Sandy, my name doesn't seem unusual to me at all. I've always worn it like a sign that tells people what I expect of them … and of myself."

Even though she smiled politely, I could tell that young Sandy's mind had taken a detour in its quest to figure out exactly what I meant.

"Excuse me," I said. "Who's gonna see this interview?"

"Didn't Roberta give you all the information?" Sandy blinked several question marks.

"Yes, she did, but I lost track of the details."

The one detail I knew about Sandy was that she wasn't one of *Roberta's* close friends. If she were, she would have referred to *Roberta* by her middle name, Lenah. That's the name Roberta prefers. Sometimes I slip and call Lenah, Roberta. I know she forgives me when that happens because she remembers the girl I knew a long time ago went by *Roberta*.

I couldn't keep myself from smiling whenever I thought about Roberta-Lenah and our brief history. Before I'd known it, Roberta insisted on stopping by my house almost every day on her way home from school. She'd wanted to *assist* me with my work. She had questions about everything under the sun and answers to most of my questions about her and her kin, especially about the two men in her life, her father and uncle. I always knew when I'd asked her a question she didn't want to answer. She'd change the subject, or ask *me* a question.

A few years after she went back up North and found a safer space to finish growing up, Roberta started writing me letters. By then, she knew she could trust me with *her* truths because they were *mine* as well.

Sandy's voice broke into my memories.

"Everyone who comes to visit the Southern Lesbian Herstories Exhibit will have an opportunity to view the video and listen to your interview," she said.

"And where did you say the exhibit will be?"

"It'll be a traveling exhibit. So far, we have dates in St. Petersburg, Atlanta, Memphis, Richmond, and Asheville."

"What about Texas? You gonna show it there?"

"Maybe in Austin or Dallas, but we haven't finalized those arrangements."

I trusted the stool's ability to handle me shifting my weight forward and pulled up my voice from the deepest part of my chest.

"Are you from the South, Sandy?" I asked.

"No. I'm from Boston."

"Do you know anything about Texas?"

"Not from personal experience," she said.

"Well, do me a favor. Keep my part of your exhibit the hell out of Texas."

Sandy offered a sympathetic smile.

"Believe me, I understand. There's some of Texas in Boston. Taking the exhibit to Texas is probably a lousy idea, although we need to be mindful of all the lesbians who call Texas their home."

I pressed my upper lip into my lower one.

"Okay," said Sandy. "We're ready to begin."

I didn't know whether to look at the camera embedded in the little i-thing computer, or at Sandy. I decided I'd alternate.

"How long have you lived in this town, Mz. Henderson?"

"All of my life. And you can call me Myjoy or Mz. Myjoy."

"How did you make your living, Mz. Myjoy?"

"I earned my income based upon the faith people had in me."

It was only her second question, but Mz. Sandy seemed confused by my answer. Maybe she didn't have much background information about me and my life.

"Were you a religious leader, a pastor?" she asked.

"No, I was a healer."

Sandy blinked. "A doctor or a nurse?"

"No, honey. A healer. People came to my door when they had aches, pains, injuries, or they just didn't feel like themselves. The herbs and vitamins I gave them — plus the time I took to just listen to each person carefully — usually cured them."

"Would you say you were practicing medicine and pharmacology without having a license for either?"

"Nope. I wouldn't say that at all, especially because you're recording everything I'm telling you. But rest assured, there's barely a family living in this town whose members haven't crossed my threshold in search of healing. Every single one of them believed I could do it."

"And how have you dealt with folks since the Covid Pandemic started?"

"I had to stop seeing people who had fevers or coughs or the ones who felt like they had the flu. I put a sign on my door directing them to the doc-in-the-box place that's not far from here. Turning them away from my door hurt their feelings. Mine too. I was able to keep helping the ones who I knew had arthritis or muscle sprains or minor injuries."

"Are you a midwife as well as a healer?"

"No. Being pregnant and giving birth are matters that don't always turn out the way you want, and I never wanted to risk losing two people at once. There are three midwives within walking distance of everyone who lives here, though."

"That's very interesting."

Sandy nodded and drew out the four syllables of "interesting" as if she'd just stumbled upon a previously unknown anthropology study, like the backstory of the film "Daughters of the Dust," or a paragraph written by Margaret Mead about South Pacific islanders' family structures.

Yeah, I'd watched Julie Dash's movie several times and gotten lost in its beauty. And I'd read about Margaret Mead. Here, in what Roberta/Lenah used to call "Dumbfuck, Alabama," we might lack college degrees, but we sure have brains and more importantly, curiosity. We also have a public library.

"Let's turn to another topic, Mz. Myjoy." Sandy recovered from her "time-out."

"Okay, let's," I said.

"You've been an out lesbian for most of your adult life."

"Yes, I have."

"How has your community treated you all these years?"

I looked directly at the camera because I wanted to be very clear during this part of my interview.

"Mostly, I've been treated well. People my age might not have understood my attraction to women, but they taught their children to be polite and respectful to me. And when those children grew up, most of them taught their children the same thing."

"That's remarkable … and a bit unexpected." Sandy tilted her head.

"Once in a while," I continued," I'd run into a teenager with a smart mouth who'd try to scare or shame me by calling me outta' my name."

"How did you handle that?" Sandy squinted her concern.

"Oh, I'd just smile. I knew they were hiding their true selves behind their angry words, and that one day either they'd own up to who they were or die from the inside out trying to deny it."

"Mz. Myjoy, I'm going to pause here for a second." Sandy stopped filming. "My next few questions might result in you naming other individuals. As far as you know, will that be alright?"

"I'm not worried about that, not now anyway."

Sandy smiled at me and resumed the interview.

"Have you had significant relationships with women?"

"No, honey. I had *a significant relationship with one woman.*"

"Can you talk about that?"

I let the stool's curved back support me and closed my eyes for a few seconds. What could I tell her about the truest love of my life? What words could I find to describe that person? I decided to start at our beginning.

"I met Suzanne forty years ago when she moved here to be closer to the school where she taught English. She and her kindness burst into my life like jolts of sunshine after a hard rainstorm."

"What's she like?"

"She's the kindest, most considerate person I've ever

known and she's the most beautiful, inside and out." I paused. "I shoulda' brought her picture with me to show you."

Sandy smiled. "It's not too late for that. I can add a picture to the video. If you have a few photos of the two of you together, that would be great."

"Okay, I'll bring them to you."

"How did you and Suzanne first meet?"

"This is a small town. Everyone knows when a person leaves voluntarily or by divine design, and we sure know when someone new moves in. I knew who she was the first time I saw her. She was taking an evening walk. I watched her taking her strolls for a couple of weeks, but we were not within speaking distance. Then, one evening when the air laid so heavy it threatened to smother every one of my breaths, I heard her call my name. I walked towards her and looked at her close up for the very first time."

"And?"

"Oh, Jesus who art in heaven! That woman held me *and* infinity in her eyes!"

"That sounds like a powerful first meeting."

"It was a 'hello, I've been waiting for you for a long time' first meeting. The thing is, until that moment I never knew I'd been waiting for someone. Suzanne said she hadn't known she'd been waiting also. There were two other towns close to her school, but she just happened to choose this one."

"When did you decide to live together?"

"Not right away. We were afraid she'd lose her job, and she loved teaching almost as much as she loved us being together. After a while we said the hell with it. If the school's administrators found out that Suzanne and I lived together, so be it. Life is short and we deserved to live it as we pleased. As we pleased meant living under the same roof, talking about how our days had gone every evening at supper. We took turns cooking so that neither one of us would feel it was our duty," I said. "Besides, we each had favorite dishes we liked to prepare."

"And by sharing that task, neither of you was saddled with a prescribed role," Sandy said.

"Right ... but it wasn't all thought out like that. It just happened naturally."

"Forty years is a very long to maintain a relationship."

"It doesn't seem long to us. Not nearly long enough," I said. "Have you ever gone to a party where you were having so much fun and feeling so happy that you didn't want it to end? That's how I feel about spending forty years of my life with Suzanne."

"You two are very lucky."

"We've been each other's good fortune. We've planned birthdays and Christmas celebrations together, decided jointly what we'd plant in our vegetable and herb gardens each Spring, caressed each other amid our laughter and our tears. We've marveled at and enjoyed the wonder of each other's body as the passing years changed us, and we've slept in each other's arms every night with few exceptions."

"That's almost too wonderful to believe, Mz. Myjoy."

"Oh, you'd best believe it. And it's still wonderful."

"Did Suzanne ever run into roadblocks at her school?"

"No. After a while everyone knew Suzanne and I lived

together, but she was never fired. We were lucky and the school board members had more common sense than hatred. They recognized a skillful teacher when they saw one. Years later when she retired, her school threw her a big party and they included me. They said I was Suzanne's life partner and I had every right to be there with her."

Sandy beamed as though my and Suzanne's victory had been hers as well.

"Have you retired as well, Mz. Myjoy?"

"Not really. I don't move around as quick as I used to, but as long as people need me to tend to their aches and whatnot, I'll keep working to help them heal."

"I want to thank you for giving us your time today, Mz. Myjoy."

"And I want to thank you, Sandy, for including my voice along with the other Southern Lesbian Voices in your exhibition."

Mindful of the stool's height and the distance between the ground and my feet, I eased myself out of the soft leather seat and walked toward Sandy.

"On second thought, maybe you *should* take the exhibit to Texas. It's a big state and there are more lesbians there than there are here. There are brown and black lesbians who need to hear about our past and feel hopeful about our future."

Sandy extended her hand to me.

"I believe you're right, Mz. Myjoy Henderson. I believe you're right."

I waved a good-bye to Sandy and picked up my pace, eager to get home where Suzanne was no doubt fixing one of my favorite meals ... her macaroni and cheese along with a mixture of collard and turnip greens.

Let's just get real for a minute (Dec. 14, 2022)
doris diosa davenport

it was only for fun and to be done for a few days
to try some of the ways but now my brain
is fettered to a concept of rhyme
my mind stuck (tethered?) trying to find
forgetting that there was a time when – it was only for fun.
(Come through, now.)

Rhyming or not this is still a great day!
Our "BG" is back home, safe.
Many groups and people wanted her home
but only us, only we,
black wimmin know this
deep pleasure. praise. relief.

Endless gratitude b/c the world knows what we know
that BG is articulate, gorgeous, beautiful, sensual, strong
that the whole world wants to own or to be a black womon
and when they can't even tell the truth –

instead they punish, humiliate, hurt,
instead of praise, honor and celebrate we know
how all this could have gone; we rejoice
that she is now (almost) home
with her wife and friends. To recover, to rest, to be
healed in love. And joy. (Black Female Joy.)

Let's just get real for a minute

Part 2, "keepn it real"

i will get something done today
to celebrate that Brittney Griner is on the way
(home from a prison camp in Russia Dec. 8, 2022)
It may be to just make up the bed
it could be that i comb my head it could be
i just dance and laugh instead and
i don't care if this gets read or not –
Brittney is coming home.
Brittney is coming home and Warnock won. Uh uh uh

(Can't tell me *nothing* today!)

Like Stella
After Billie Zangewa's Evelyn's Island Escape
Yeva Johnson

As if she were Stella's queer
cousin, Evelyn's ready for this vacation
break from everyday life. Kids grown,
obligations on hold, she steps out in style.
Plum roses scatter across her silk satin ruby
red robe draping her dark lanky frame
as she bats her lashes at the beautiful Black woman
she met on the beach and the highest clouds reflect
her toothsome smile – groove or no groove,
Evelyn's prepped for paradise.

Joy Delayed
Penny Mickelbury

"If you weren't one of the best visual artists in the world, I'd suggest you seek a career on the stage. You do drama quite well."

"And if you weren't the best doctor in this wretched city I'd fire you and seek another! I don't appreciate you laughing at me!"

"You'd laugh, too, if you'd seen the look of horror on your face." And Dr. Edie Miller gave her prickly patient a quick, tight hug, and returned to the swivel stool in front of her computer screen where she typed additional notes into Georgina Gale's chart.

"You told me I was old! How was I supposed to look? And you told me I needed a cane! You might as well play the death march!" Gina inhaled and caught her breath … and her temper. Dr. Miller had merely reminded Gina that she was 74 years old, as if she needed fucking reminding, and no matter what the good doctor said, 74 was old! Both her parents were dead by that age, ergo 74 was old! And what would she look like walking around with a cane!

"I said 'walking stick,' Gina, and you're an artist. Surely you know someone who could carve something magnificent for you — something that would be a work of art, something that an artist of your caliber could possess without anyone attaching age or infirmity to it." The good doctor sounded so logical and rational. And so correct.

Joy Delayed

"I'm sorry I snapped," Gina said, giving full reign to the possibility of what Dr. Miller just said. Then she frowned. "Am I dying?" Then she laughed at the look on the doctor's face.

"Why on earth would you ask such a question? Of course you're not dying! You easily may live another twenty or twenty-five years, Gina. You are in excellent health, really you are."

"Except for the arthritis throughout my body."

Dr. Miller nodded. "And I am concerned that you may lose your balance and take a tumble —"

"Fall on my ass, you mean," Gina snapped. The anger was back and this time Dr. Miller didn't ignore it, and Gina replayed her words and the attendant warning over and over for the remainder of that day and night, and well into the following morning, when she bought a cane at the chain drugstore, then visited Khadijah, her sculptor friend, and commissioned a carved walking stick. She was calmed by the thought of holding on to the orishas and ancestors, of them supporting her as she made her way through her world. A world that age and infirmity would compress into ever narrower boundaries with every passing year, assuming that she really would live another 20 or 25 years.

We can't cure arthritis, or limit it, but we can manage it and the pain it causes. And one of the best ways to do that is to keep it moving, and swimming is the best exercise. Find a pool and make regular use of it. Go to the Pain Management Clinic — that's a very useful resource. And use the walking stick because a fall could be disastrous: you could break a leg, a hip, an arm, or a wrist when you put your arms out to break a fall.

Dr. Miller had intended her words as a cautionary tale. Gina heard a more dire warning but she hadn't the time for more than one visit to the pain management clinic, and she had no time for swimming. She had a gallery show to prepare for and she was the featured artist. No, dammit she wasn't old or dead! At least for now.

Victoria Creighton didn't like crowds but she did like Georgina Gale's art — she had two of her earlier paintings but none of the recent works, which were larger in scale and complexity and considerably more expensive. Vic also was liking her pseudo girlfriend less by the minute — thirty of them at this point. The woman was of the mistaken belief that keeping someone waiting induced a longing response in that person. It induced a kiss-my-ass response in Vic. She turned off her phone, shoved it into her back pocket, and eased into the crowded gallery. It was new, spacious, and of necessity well-lit, for which Vic was grateful. There were pockets of people arrayed in front of various displays, none of which were works by Georgina Gale, and those were the only works of interest to Vic. Then she spied the objects of her interest across the room and headed in that direction, glad that the congestion dictated that she move forward slowly and deliberately.

Vic was no art connoisseur, she was a numbers cruncher, and a very good one. Among the best, truth be told. There was beauty in numbers, but there was no color. She began visiting museums and galleries initially for the color. Then she realized and understood that there was a symmetry to art, that it was numbers with color, and she bought her first painting. Then she discovered Georgina Gale and a new level of appreciation for art. She liked Gina Gale's work the way she liked Augusta Savage and Betye Saar and Elizabeth Catlett: Because they spoke to her, aroused feelings and thoughts and reactions within her. Then she discovered that she and Gina lived in the same city and were alumnae of the same university and Vic became a collector of Gina Gale's work. Collector with a small c, because Gina Gale, overnight it seemed, became one of the most popular painters not just in America but in the world. And overnight it seemed to Vic, she became more and more aware of her compromised vision. More than 30 years of scrutinizing rows and columns and ledgers of numbers were taking their toll. There was no way to reverse the damage already done, Vic's doctor said, but she could slow its progress. How? Vic asked eagerly. Get a new profession, was the doctor's advice. Sure, Vic had replied, that's exactly what I'll do at 63 years of age! I'll get a new profession! Maybe I'll go to med school!

Vic made her way through the crowd to the section of the gallery dedicated solely to Gina Gale's work. Most people were standing a little away, as one did, to fully view the art, but Vic got closer so she could see the prices: could she afford anything? Two of the larger pieces already boasted SOLD stickers beside them at prices Vic could never afford, and even if she could, no wall in her house was large enough to accommodate them. But two of the smaller pieces ... the colors so intense and dramatic they leapt off the canvas.

She hurried toward them, her phone already in her hand, the camera on and ready. She pressed and held the button and moved the camera about so that she captured many images. Then a man was hurrying toward her, smiling and exchanging greetings along the way. Must be the gallery owner, Vic thought, and was proved correct when he stuck a SOLD label on the wall beside one of the paintings. Vic was shooting photos again and she was really glad because she didn't believe what she'd just witnessed: the gallery owner quickly and surreptitiously changed the price of the picture! Still smiling he turned and faced the crowd. Had anyone witnessed what he did? The new price lowered the original price by $10,000, which meant he'd just cheated Gina Gale out of $10,000.

Camera still in her hand, hand in her pocket, Vic photographed all the Gina Gale paintings and their prices. The artist would know what the prices should be, wouldn't she? Or her dealer would? Viv had no idea how the art world worked and she didn't know who to ask. But what she did know was numbers: She was a forensic accountant and if she could get her hands on the gallery's books ... but how would she do that?

The energy in the gallery suddenly shifted, and there was a buzz, as if a gentle electrical current pulsed through the room. Then there was applause and cheers. Then the crowd parted and there was Gina Gale and Vic's breath caught in her chest. What a magnificent woman! She'd only seen photographs, never the artist in person, moving with regal elegance through the crowd supported by a carved walking stick that even from a distance of several feet Vic could tell was an artistic masterpiece. Then the crowd closed around Gina and Vic knew there'd be no way to get close enough to explain to the artist what she'd seen and what she believed was happening. And even if she could talk to Gina, could she convince her to believe what she was hearing? Vic thought, hoped, that she must know someone who had an artist as a client. Surely someone who produced and sold a product all over the world, one costing many thousands of dollars, needed a skilled accountant to keep track of things.

"Creative types as a rule don't spend time watching the bottom line, which is why you hear about so many of 'em getting ripped off by managers and agents." Vic's friend Dave crunched numbers at one of the largest and most well-respected accounting firms in town. His clients were all musicians and he didn't think the firm represented any visual artists. "But I do know the only way to get their attention is to suggest they'll be broke if they don't start paying attention to what they earn." And he secured Gina Gale's address for her.

Vic's letter to Gina was comprehensive yet succinct, and fully factual, supported by the videos she shot at the gallery opening night the previous weekend. Vic also included the name of the best lawyer she knew — Lucille Smythe — and strongly suggested that Gina contact and consult her. She had the sealed package delivered to Gina's studio by a private courier. And then Vic's world exploded and collapsed on her and around her and she could think about nothing else.

Though they didn't know it, had no way of knowing it, Vic and Gina were experiencing similar emotional upheavals over the next thirteen months: time both expanded, then compressed and then halted, before speeding up and spinning events out of their control. Which was just as well because neither of them would have wanted to think deeply about what they were going through, nor would they have possessed the strength, emotional or physical, to deal with it.

Gina emerged first, still a bit shaky but able to begin forward movement. Studying the card she held, called Victoria Creighton's office and asked to speak with her. She didn't immediately understand what she heard: Victoria Creighton was no longer there, she now longer owned the company, she sold it almost a year ago.

"But if you need an accountant ..."

"No, I don't. I need to locate Victoria Creighton."

"You can probably find her at the construction company."

"Construction company?" Gina asked, puzzled and confused."

"Creighton General Contractors."

A vague recognition ... then a sudden flash of memory: Two men killed in a building collapse on a construction site a year or so ago ... men named Creighton! She stood up quickly, too quickly, and lost her balance. She hit the floor hard and she lay there for a long moment, scanning her body for a sign of serious injury. Finding none she rolled onto her side and using her desk chair for support, she levered herself up and into the chair. She grabbed the phone, and called Cille Smythe, the best lawyer Vic said she knew, who now also was Gina's good and trusted friend and a shark of a lawyer.

"Gina, is anything wrong?" Cille said by way of a greeting.

"I just called Vic, or thought I was calling Vic ... Cille, those two men killed when the building collapsed on that construction site last year ..."

"Vic's father and brother."

Suddenly Gina was weeping though she didn't know why. She didn't know Vic Creighton, had never met her — this woman whose concern and kindness had stopped people she had liked, respected, trusted, from stealing everything from her. Cille and three forensic accountants from Vic's office — her former office — uncovered and proved how Gina's dealer and gallery conspired and colluded to defraud her of hundreds of thousands, if not millions, of dollars, not only by falsifying sales prices (as Vic's videos proved), but by keeping Gina's work out of certain gallery shows in Europe. And now this woman was dealing with such a horrible and painful tragedy.

"You should call her, Gina. She'd really like hearing from you."

"She doesn't know me, Cille, and I don't know her."

"But you each have deep respect and regard for the other, and you've both been through hell. I think you need each other."

Gina was glad Cille couldn't see the glare she threw at the phone, but the lawyer didn't need to see it. She knew her prickly client-friend and a slow grin spread across her face. She knew what was coming. "You haven't the slightest idea what I need … OK … maybe you have a slight idea, but Cille, I can't just call a woman I don't know!"

"Since you don't call the ones you do know, why not try something new," Cille said, and disconnected. Gina's pique took a back seat as she wondered how Lucille Smythe knew whom she called or didn't call or, for that matter, whom she knew. Then she sighed and allowed common sense and good manners to take over. A call to Victoria Creighton was long overdue if for no other reason than to thank her. She made the call.

"Miss Gale! What a pleasant surprise. To what do I owe the honor?"

"I should have called you long before now, Miss Creighton, and I'm truly sorry that I didn't."

"You had a few things on your mind, and please call me Vic."

"On my mind was how do I ever find the words to thank you for what you did for me, and what words can I use to express my sorrow at the loss of your family. I cannot imagine the depth of your grief."

Now Vic was at a loss for words. None had so closely touched what she felt — not people she had known all her life, not people she was related to. She remembered her friend Dave telling her that artists were different from what he called 'us regular people.' And when Vic had pressed for an explanation he'd said that the run-of-the-mill artistic types often were self-centered, childish, and boorish. But what he called 'the genuine articles,' — people like Gina Gale — were in direct communication with the angels. *Think about what you see and feel when you look at her paintings.*

Joy Delayed

Why do we still listen to Roberta Flack and Nina Simone?
Vic understood Dave then and thanks to him, she understood
Gina Gale now. "Thank you, Miss Gale."

"Please call me Gina, and please allow me to thank you
properly—"

"If you'll allow me to treat you to dinner. Tonight."

A moment of stunned silence allowed both women to
regain a modicum of control, though neither was, truth be
told, in control of the moment, and neither was accustomed
to being caught on the back foot. Given adequate time and
distance from the moment both likely would find some
amusement in it. Not now, however. "I apologize if that was
too forward," Vic said.

"Not at all," Gina replied with an almost smile, which
was unexpectedly followed by more truth: "It's been a while
since I was invited to dinner so I was a bit taken aback."

"Then if you'll accept having me pick up dinner, then
having me pick you up, then hanging out at my place, it's a
date!" Vic practically choked on the word. She hadn't had a
date in — she didn't know how long, and she was one eye
exam away from a white cane and a Braille lesson. How
would she explain that to a woman whose vision informed
her livelihood?

Gina quickly agreed and even more quickly disconnected the call. Whatever was she doing! What was she
thinking? A date! With a woman she barely knew, despite
the debt of gratitude she owed her. She could barely walk
most days and the only effective pain medication made her
a zombie. She hadn't acknowledged the truth to herself but
perhaps it was time: she was finished as a painter, and she

had no grounds for complaint. She'd had a hell of a career, and with thanks to Vic Creighton and Lucille Smythe, she was what once was called filthy rich (as opposed to clean rich?). And she had a date, which she remembered enough about to know required that she shower and dress ... nicely.

Alejandro, who once drove her 80+ year old parents everywhere — and they were always on the go — now drove Vic to pick up dinner and her date and back home, which was a guest house at the rear of her parents' house. As she helped Gina out of the car, she was surprised how heavily the artist leaned on her, and she realized that the intricately carved stick was not an affectation or a prop. She put an around Gina's waist, then withdrew it.

"Is that painful? I don't want to hurt you."

"My ribs are about the only bones in my body that aren't arthritic," Gina said. "But if I could lean on your shoulder with my left arm, while my right hand holds the stick ...?"

"And if your eyes can guide us up the path to my house ...?"

And with Alejandro bringing up the rear with the food and the wine, they got to the house and inside. They decided where Gina would be most comfortable, and that's where they ate. The gas fire provided both warmth against the always chilly Los Angeles evening, and an always welcome ambiance. The food — Greek, Indian, and Thai — from Vic's favorite restaurants, was delicious, as was the Proseco. They ate all the food, including the baklava, and drank almost all the wine. They talked about everything and laughed about a great many things, including the fact that they had a similar sense of humor. They enjoyed discovering that they both were UCLA grads albeit a decade apart, and then silence reigned when each confessed that age and infirmity meant acknowledging that their careers were, for all intents and purposes, over.

"Are you comfortable with that?" Gina asked Vic.

"I don't know about comfortable but I suppose I'm accepting because I have no choice. I need my sight to do my job. And I really don't care to be here without my family." Vic took a breath and placed the focus on Gina. "And you? Are you comfortable with the idea of no longer being able to create masterpieces?"

"Well … when you put it that way," Gina replied with dry sarcasm. "I've been offered teaching jobs, so maybe I'll teach until the grim reaper comes for me. How about you? What will you do, Vic?"

Then Vic told Gina what she'd told no one else: "I'm moving to St. Croix while I can still see. The sunrises and sunsets over the Caribbean, and the blues and greens of the water."

Gina gave her a steady look but when she spoke it wasn't in response to Vic's announcement, it was to ask for help standing up and for directions to the bathroom. Vic took both her hands and pulled her to her feet, then held her tightly until she steadied. Then she and the walking stick provided support to the bathroom, but only the walking stick entered with her, and Vic hurried back to the living room and began clearing away. When she looked toward the bathroom she found that Gina was watching her and she went to help her return to her place of comfort on the sofa. "Why St.

Croix?" she asked as soon as she was settled.

"Because it's beautiful and peaceful, and because I have no history and no memories there." And suddenly she was weeping, wailing. And as if there was no crippling arthritis in her body, Gina Gale reached for Vic, pulled her close, and held her as she wept. Wept like the child who suddenly realizes she's alone in the world with no parents or siblings, and Gina wondered if this was the first time Vic had cried since the loss of her family.

When finally she was all cried out, Vic pushed herself up into a sitting position. "I need to go wash my face and blow my nose," she said, "and then come to apologize to you. And I'll bring you a shirt to change into since I've cried and snotted all over the one you're wearing."

"No apology is necessary, Vic, and I mean that. I'm glad I was here for you. As for the tears and snot — nothing but salt and water — and hurry back so we can discuss that."

Vic, nose blown and face washed, hurried back with a tee shirt for Gina to change into. "Not as pretty as the blouse you're wearing but at least it's dry."

Without a word Gina unbuttoned the blouse, removed it, and exchanged it for the tee shirt. Vic almost missed the exchange because Gina wasn't wearing a bra and Vic barely stopped herself from verbally emoting. "Sorry if I caused you any embarrassment," Gina said, pulling the tee shirt over her head, then leaning forward so that Vic could lift the thick, heavy ropes of dreadlocks that cascaded down Gina's back out of the way.

"You definitely caused a reaction but it wasn't embarrassment," Vic said with a chuckle. "So, what was it you wanted to discuss?"

"About St. Croix … is it all right to ask you about it? Are you all right talking about it?"

"More than all right," Vic responded, and proved it by telling Gina everything she knew, felt, and thought about St. Croix in particular, and the U.S. Virgin Islands in general. "I'm going there in a few days since I have no home, no job, no office, no family, and no real reason to be here. You should come with me. The warm Caribbean sun and the warm salt water of the Caribbean Ocean are healing and therapeutic."

"Are you coming back?" Gina asked, with an arched right eyebrow.

"This time," Vic responded with a lopsided, rakish grin.

"I'm a new woman, thanks to you and to the healing properties of the Caribbean Sea and sun," Gina said as they relaxed on the terrace of Vic's newly constructed home nestled on a hillside above the blue-green waters. The soothing afternoon breeze belied the quasi-brutal heat of midday, and Gina initially resisted Vic's efforts to get her out of the sun and the water and into the house at midday. "You've heard the phrase, 'mad dogs and Englishmen?' Then you no doubt know the reference?" Vic pressed the issue until Gina, practically on the verge of sunstroke, capitulated. So they swam from around 8:00 am until about 11:30 am when Lindy drove them back up the hill to Vic's, where they showered and rested and enjoyed a midday meal.

"Are you saying I have healing properties?" Vic asked innocently.

"My body was so focused on relieving the arthritis pain that it wasn't aware how much I needed other kinds of relief, which you provide with breathtaking expertise." She chuckled. Then, after a beat, added, "I'm so glad I'm not dead!"

Vic choked on her lemonade and Gina got up to clap her on the back. She balanced herself on Vic's shoulders and on the backs on their chairs but her movement was so much steadier now, as was her confidence. "I'm kinda glad you're not dead, too." In fact Vic was overjoyed. She could never have imagined it possible that she could or would find such a powerful yet beautiful love like Gina Gale at this stage of her life, and she knew that Gina felt the same way about her. Nobody thought about or wrote about women finding love in their 60s and 70s, and they couldn't be the only ones, so why the secrecy? But perhaps it was better this way: Nobody watching two old women enjoying life would ever imagine just how much enjoyment was involved!

Gina remained standing behind Vic, massaging her neck and shoulders, an activity that was oddly soothing to her arthritic hands and fingers. Lindy and Mattie came out to the terrace to clear away the dishes and to shoo away the bold little sandpipers always on the lookout for a bite to eat. The two women were more than household help to Vic: Banished from their homes on the island of St. Thomas because they loved each other instead of their husbands, they fled to St. Croix where they sought refuge in Vic's under-construction house. Recognizing kindred spirits Vic hired them with the promise of work and a place to live when the house was finished, and she kept that promise. And Lindy and Mattie took care of Gina and Vic like family. In fact the four women were family.

When they were alone again Gina raised the issue she'd been avoiding: their return to Los Angeles in a week. Vic really didn't need to go. Gina really did: she needed to finalize the sale of the two buildings she owned, one which housed her studios and where she rented space to other artists, the other which housed the loft where she lived and where she rented similar space. She not only never wanted to return to LA, she never wanted to leave St. Croix. But they both also needed to see their doctors, both of whom promised to have referrals in St. Croix.

"Please promise me, Vic, that we won't need to stay longer than a week."

"Lucille not only has everything in hand, but she's coming back here with us, so we won't be staying longer than a week," Vic said, changing the subject to a discussion of the things they would do to entertain Cille. They wanted to share every aspect of the joy of their lives with the woman who was so much more than their lawyer. They wanted her to see firsthand the proof that joy delayed was not joy diminished or reduced by the number of one's birthdays — but enhanced by that fact. Joy delayed was joy appreciated.

The Spirit of the Rhythm Catches You and You Dance

Maria Hamilton Abegunde

What might our writing look like if it were imbued with characters and themes centered on joy and delight?

Unwittingly, this question invites me to describe something I have experienced but rarely testify on: Myself in the throes of joy. It affirms how I welcome writing about joy and delight as process, embodiment, and outcome. For me, both are personal, spontaneous, and childlike.

The question invites me to consider why I write. I am alive because I write. I write because I am alive. Writing helps me bring awareness to the quiddity of my everyday existence with reverence and awe no matter how mundane.

My writing is a practice dedicated to joy's "…constant unfolding…" and "…the way and work of blackness, an unfolding that is simultaneously an enfolding" (Crawley, 148 and 147).

||

1982. Joy brings me to a quiet place, in the upper room of my dormitory. I am on the floor. I vacillate between stillness and dancing. Such joy delights me to the point of bliss. I am rendered silent, unable to articulate anything but Love through movement.

The Spirit of the Rhythm Catches You and You Dance

Joy: Overwhelming and sustained happiness generated from within oneself through connection with something greater than oneself.

Delight: The pleasure and satisfaction one receives from this feeling.

||

The question declares Blackness as an inherent part of my being and has freed me from doing what is often expected and demanded of Black writers: To explain being Black or to expound upon resistance.

Joy: When unburdened by perspectives and mandates to perform Black/ness, I can *be* Black, unconstructed and unbound by borders and boundaries. And, what delight I have in the things I ponder when I am free.

Yesterday: Breath, breathing. Om. Today: A ruby-throated hummingbird hovered in front of my face. Tomorrow: What is "space"? In my dreams: I am dancing to Chaka Khan's *Like Sugar* (so sweet). Right now: I want to write about what happens when the music plays.

||

So, what might our writing look like if it were imbued with characters and themes centered on joy and delight?

Questions beget questions. Why should I not contemplate my relationships with the joy, pleasure, bliss that comes from meeting myself in what I hold holy: My body untethered to time or place and full of sound.

Maria Hamilton Abegunde

I am an unfolding being, enfolded by joy, especially when I am dancing.

||

2019. A Monday night in Rio de Janeiro. I am at a *samba das trabalhadoras* in one of the oldest samba clubs in the city. This samba honors the everyday lives of working people, who come from all over Rio to dance. I arrived with my students and colleagues. This is our night together, away from the academic study of Black life in Rio, and into the circle of living it. And, dearly beloved, who among us would say that the club dance floor is not a sacred and holy site of transformation and, when the music and company are on point, one of transmigration?

This night, one of the most revered samba players in the city turned to me and asked in Portuguese, *a senhora, did you like the music?* I approached the stage after the first set to thank him. It was then that I noticed what was not evident when he played: The shaking of his hands, his difficulty speaking when he stood still without his guitar.

His question is a petition for a blessing. *A senhora, did you like the music?* It is the way he approaches me with a reverence given to a senior priest: Stepping back, not looking at me directly, bowing slightly, and speaking in a near whisper. *Ah, sim, o senhor.* Yes, I tell him, very much, thank you for the music. He smiles and offers me one of his CDs. I take it gratefully and graciously, and touch his body before returning to the dance floor. He does not flinch. His body remains still under my hand.

The Spirit of the Rhythm Catches You and You Dance

We stand in a hall surrounded by murals of community ancestors. *O povo,* the people, are sharing food with each other, even with us strangers, in corners of the room as if we are at a picnic on the beach. They playfully challenge the students to dance and to show off what they have been learning in samba class. The women laugh with me and call me *querida,* dear one. They all think I am a *Baiana* from Salvador and speak to me in Portuguese. The men smile and move out of my way. The old ones with more confidence ask permission to dance with me.

O senhor does not know I am not Brazilian. It does not matter. He knows I am a healer and a priest, and that neither has stopped me from enjoying his music with my full self. We have seen each other come alive through what we love most and what fills us with such ecstasy that our frailties disappear long enough for us to witness something sacred moving through us: The samba. He plays uninhibited by his body, perhaps fueled by his genetic memories of younger days. And me, I dance unabashedly like when I was a child, free within myself. I do not care that one of my students took a photo so close that you can count the beads of sweat rolling down my neck.

It is always like this for me. Music, dancing, moving with sound and rhythm. I am freest, most Black and, therefore, joyful when I am dancing, surrounded by no one, or those who also find themselves stepping into notes that will undo the tensions knotted into our muscles and nerves.

In these moments, I struggle to remain present. Every molecule in me wants to escape from the confines and limitations of skin. My bones want to return to stardust. I imagine what is left of me falling to the floor, eventually disappearing into the dirt beneath me.

When I become aware that my body threatens to implode, reconstitute itself, then explode, this is when I close my eyes, as if doing so will bind ligaments and blood. This is when I believe that if I don't hold myself tightly I will disintegrate. To remain whole, I throw my head back, hold my breath, open my mouth, and begin to shrill, the sound my spirit makes when it turns my body inside out for everyone to see.

Instead of fighting the music or the disintegration of my bones, I let the music undo my insistence to remain who I was when I stepped onto the floor. I allow myself to float. I understand how small and infinite I am; how ravenous I am for unity with the Universe, which has no center and is fluid. All of me, beginning with those beads of sweat, flow into the nothingness that surrounds me.

When people say you are glowing, it is not your sweat cascading down your face. It is your soul covering your skin. What they are seeing is joy, raw and purified.

||

This type of dancing, in public, eyes closed like I am in worship reminds me that I am one with the One. When I think of separation from what I deem as sacred in my daily life – cooking a good meal, laughing, loving – I think of how it's impossible for me to separate my Blackwomanness from my writing, creating, and living, and how their connection helps me dwell in the "what if" between the sacred and profane, the extraordinary and quotidian.

What is the point of joy, if not to treat the ordinary moments of our lives as ceremony; to reach down deep into the center of one's heart and soul, the places that cannot be taken unless we willingly open our bodies, ourselves, reveal what is hidden, and give what we find there to others?

II

As a child, I sought this experience of sharing what moved me before understanding why when I heard music I would get up, close my eyes, and dance around a room with a spontaneously choreographed dance.

1972. *Imagine there's no heaven / it's easy if you try / no hell below us / above us, only sky / imagine all the people / living for today … living life in peace … … you may say I'm a dreamer …* (John Lennon, 1971).

I rise from the couch and step into the center of the living room floor. As if on cue, everyone forms a circle around me and my body moves – more than 40 years later, I know that I was moving but I cannot say that I moved. What I know then: John Lennon wrote this song for me. It will be decades before I can embody its promise in my own work as a healer, poet, and priest. But, in this moment I whirl, covering all parts of the room with such urgency that I do not have time to think about what I am doing, or why.

I am not yet eight years old. Writing poetry is already saving my life. And, dancing is teaching me how to be free. Something in me knows that John Lennon is writing about the possibility of a union that I desire but cannot name. As soon as the song begins, it stops, and I return to my seat, as if nothing happened. My onlookers clap while I wonder how I can create this world where I dance whenever I want to, and where peace is possible.

||

1970. August and it is carnival time in Grenada, my mother's home island, the place I still call home. My mother, her youngest sister, and I leave our home parish of St. Patrick and travel to Grenville.

I remember looking out of someone's apartment window and seeing people in costumes and dancing in the street. I remember following the sound of steel drums and calypso and running from my mother and aunt. I remember that they were relieved when they found me. What I do not remember is how I got on the small stage.

But, I know that I can dance. What I don't know, but will learn as I grow older: When the rhythm begins, it compels me to put aside all of body and mind – anything that disrupts communication between the vibrations emitting from us both; call and response, but whose doing which is still not clear. Surrender is not easy. Yet, my desire to be filled-up by an unimaginable pleasure overrides any fear I may have. I want the joy. I want the unification of all things sentient and Black. I want to be free.

||

The Spirit of the Rhythm Catches You and You Dance

2006. I do not know it yet, but this is the year that defines and reveals who I am when I am unafraid to let the rhythm shake me.

I am on stage with Dobet Gnahore, Vusi Mahlasela, and Habib Koite. Their drummer saw me. As I turned counterclockwise, he put down his drum, and by the time I am facing front again, he has taken my hand to guide me through the audience and towards the stage.

Later, I will call my father and tell him excitedly that I danced for three of Africa's best-known musicians. It is he who taught me it was okay to "jump up" in the street, in a restaurant – any place – when the rhythm gets going good. I will tell him how Dobet Gnahore, the most physically powerful dancer I have ever seen, crouched down to look at my feet. And how Vusi and Habib played for me as if we all knew each other.

But for now, I remove my shoes and leave them at the top of the stairs, salute each of the drums, and move like all my life I have lived for this moment. I am in complete control. But, I keep my eyes on Dobet to remember that I cannot stay in this space forever.

When I am ready to leave, I signal to the drummer who took my hand, first with one hip, then the other, winding slowly until the sound he plays mimics my movements and he follows me to the edge of the stage where I turn and bow towards him and the others.

He walks me back to my seat. The audience salutes me with applause and shouting. My elders in the front seats tell me how wonderful I was; how I have made them proud. And, now, everyone wants to dance with me, to touch me.

It is only when I return home that I realize I was not afraid. I will tell my father this: I wasn't afraid, I didn't even think about it. I held my head up, and allowed my body to publicly remember, dare I say it, home.

Backstage, after the performance, before I could thank the drummer, he takes my hands and says: I knew you could dance.

Joy: I offer to hundreds of people the part of me that is connected to an ancestral call that makes one of Africa's most incredible dancers watch how I place my feet on the wood, surrender my hips to the drumbeat, and never once drop my shoulders or neck lazily. Later, when everyone is gone, she will wait for me on stage to ask me if I am from Benin. Because, she says, I dance like those women. She will not be the last to tell me this.

In this moment, unrequested, unplanned, unexpected, I am all of me past, present, and future. I accepted the invitation to enter the circle, and chose to leave when I was satiated to a comfortable fullness and willingness to expose who I was, and aware enough to see how Dobet rested her chin on her fist, studied my movements with appreciation, and nodded as I backed carefully away from the drums.

The surprise of having no fear arrives later. For now, I move as if dancing in front of over 200 people, supported by three of Africa's most celebrated musicians from Ivory Coast, South Africa, and Mali is something I do every day.

My body does not fall apart. My muscles cling to my bones. And my bones cling to the DNA that lives in the drums. Our skins recognize each other, and we resonate in timbres and tones only the earth can hear.

The Spirit of the Rhythm Catches You and You Dance

||

I am an unfolding being, enfolded by joy, especially when I am dancing.

||

My body is a sound only the initiated can hear; only those who know can witness.

||

At rare and unexpected times during meditation when you become so still, inside and outside, you cease to exist as an individual. Your nervous system recognizes the roots under the earth, and you realize that you are connected to all of creation. You feel and hear the trees across the world talking to one another; you hear and sense the oceans flowing towards each other. A blackbird lands on you and walks across your head and shoulders. A ruby-throated hummingbird stops in front of you for what seems like minutes, but is really seconds. Your body remembers its skin responds to the skin of the drum, and that the drum sounds like your heart beating.

Only then do you know for sure that joy is buried in your heart and that unless you are willing to give that organ to someone, no one can take it from you. When this type of joy begins to erupt, it can be painful. Our bodies and psyches are not prepared for the sudden birth of such immense and incomprehensible emotions. After they pass through you, the universe blinks at you, and you feel Her vibration forever in every nerve and in every sinew that holds you together. You become alive in ways you never dreamed.

||

We do what we can do to make space for these feelings: We weep. Later, we will try to explain it to others as I have tried to do here without worry that my words are inadequate. Words can represent and not replicate the experience; they obfuscate the meaning and diffuse the power that such joy holds and inspires.

||

Imagine the endless and inevitable possibilities of Black women and girls dancing to the rhythms of their hearts, and them writing about it over their lifetimes.

||

The written word cannot fully name these joys. I have to show you. You have to hear it. We want to feel it. Still, I write because what is writing but my commitment to sharing the everydayness of spontaneous healing when least expected – and knowing that despite their limitations, the words are memories I have embedded and embodied.

||

The Spirit of the Rhythm Catches You and You Dance

"I can say I write because I am a Black immigrant woman living in a white, male dominated, racist, and classist society. But I write primarily because of a spiritual compulsion which demands that I put pen to paper and open my mouth and chant" (Cooper, 1990).

And what, you ask, does that chanting look like? All the throats of my foremothers and current mothers and sisters opening and pouring libations upon my fingers, my keyboard, my choice of pens and pencils, my papers. Their hands are drumming my body until the residue of all the lives I did not want to live is removed and written on the sun. When they are done, a hundred years ago and in the future, all that will remain will be me.

||

I am an unfolding being, enfolded by joy, especially when I am dancing.

Ase!

References

Cooper. Afua. 1990. "Finding My Voice" in *Caribbean Women Writers: Essays from the First International Conference*. Ed. Selwyn R. Cudjoe. Amherst, MA: University of Massachusetts Press.

Crawley, Ashon. 2022. *The Lonely Letters*. Durham, NC: Duke University Press.

Lennon, John. 1971. "Imagine" on the album *Imagine*. Apple Records.

CONTRIBUTORS

Dr. Maria Hamilton Abegunde is a Memory Keeper, healer, and a devotee of the *orisa* Osun. Her writings have been published in *FIRE!!, North Meridian Review, Massachusetts Review, Tupelo Quarterly, Trouble the Waters: Tales of the Deep Blue, Ashe: Ritual Poetics in African Diasporic Expressivity*, and *SO WE CAN KNOW: Writers of Color on Pregnancy, Loss, Abortion*, and *Birth*. She is the commissioned poet for *Be/Coming, Keeper of My Mothers' Dreams*, and *Sister Song* exhibitions. She is a Cave Canem and Black Earth Institute (BEI) fellow. She is a faculty member in the Department of African American and African Diaspora Studies.

Ashia Ajani is an award-winning Black storyteller and environmental educator originally from Denver, CO, Queen City of the Plains and the unceded territory of the Cheyenne, Ute, Arapahoe and Comanche peoples. They are a 2022 Just Buffalo Literary Fellow and a 2022 PEN America Emerging Voices Fellowship Finalist. Their words have been featured in *Hennepin Review, Apogee Journal, Exposition Review, Frontier Poetry, Them.us* and *Sierra Magazine*, among others. Their debut poetry collection, *Heirloom*, is forthcoming spring 2023 with Write Bloody Publishing.

Stephane Andrea Allen, Ph.D. is an interdisciplinary humanities scholar, creative writer, small press publisher, and Assistant Professor of Gender Studies at Indiana University. Her research centers Black lesbian cultural histories and Black feminisms through various expressions, including literature, film, and other print and visual media. Dr. Allen is also Publisher and Editor-in-Chief at BLF Press, and co-editor of *Serendipity Literary Magazine*. Her creative work can be found in various online and print publications, including *The Black Femme Collective*, *Mom Egg Review*, *Star*Line*, *Inkwell Black*, *Big Echo: Critical Science Fiction Magazine*, *Sinister Wisdom*, and in her two short story collections, *A Failure to Communicate* and *How to Dispatch a Human: Stories and Suggestions*.

Elvis Alves's latest book is *Blackfish* (Salmon Poetry, 2022). He lives in New York City with his family.

Keisha-Gaye Anderson is a Jamaican-born poet and visual artist based in Brooklyn, NY. She is the author of the poetry collections *Gathering the Waters*, *Everything is Necessary*, and *A Spell for Living*. Keisha is a past participant of VONA and Callaloo writing workshops and was short listed for the Small Axe Literary award. In 2018, she was selected as a Brooklyn Public Library Artist in Residence. She was presented with the Poetic Icon Award from her alma mater Syracuse University in 2021. Keisha holds an MFA from The City College, CUNY. Learn more about her writing and art at www.keishagaye.ink.

A former World Language teacher, **S. Renée Bess** is the author of five novels, the co-story collector of the GCLS' 2018 Goldie Award winning anthology, *Our Happy Hours, LGBT Voices from the Gay Bars,* and a series of blogs found here: thewidewindow.com. Her most recent book is *Between a Rock and a Soft Place,* a collection of short fiction, poetry, and non-fiction opinion pieces. Visit her website for more information: reneebess.com.

Àjọkẹ́ Bọdúndé is a Nigerian writer and editor. Through poetry, she aims to engage in conversations around gender, power, societal structures, and exclusion. Her work explores the experiences of women, their complex and multigenerational relationships with one another, and the patriarchy. In 2017, her poem "Girl" was published in *Aké Review*. In 2019, she was shortlisted for the Merky New Writers' Prize. She is a part of the inaugural BORN::FREE writer's collective in London, UK.

A. Brown is an Indianapolis-based writer from coastal Virginia. She writes about Black folk, for Black folk. She was a TED Residency Finalist in 2018 and a recipient of the Martha's Vineyard Institute of Creative Writing Author Fellowship. She has an MFA from Butler University, and her work has been published in *The Prism*, *RueScribe*, and *Entropy Magazine*. She is currently the Head of Editorial Content at Concept Moon and recently launched their *Concept Moon Literary Magazine*.

Lauren Cherelle uses her time and talents to traverse imaginary and professional worlds. She holds a BFA in graphic design, an MBA from the University of Tennessee, and writing certifications from the University of Louisville. Her co-edited projects include *Lez Talk: A Collection of Black Lesbian Short Fiction*, *Solace: Writing, Refuge, and LGBTQ Women of Color*, *Black from the Future: A Collection of Black Speculative Writing*, and *Sinister Wisdom: 122*. Her writing reflects the lives of Southern Black girls and women.

Esperanza Cintrón is the author of *Shades: Detroit Love Stories*, a 2020 Michigan Notable Book. Published in *Obsidian*, her story "Shadow Dancer" was nominated for a Pushcart Prize. She has four books of poetry. *What Keeps*

Me Sane won the 2013 Naomi Long Madgett Award and the most recent, *Boulders, Detroit Nature Poems,* was published by *Chestnut Review Press* in January 2023. Her work appears in a number of anthologies including *Manteca! An Anthology of Afro-Latin@ Poets*. She was awarded Callaloo Writing Fellowships at Brown and Oxford Universities; a Michigan Council for the Arts Individual Artist Grant and has a doctorate in English literature.

An undergrad at Morehouse College, **Triston Dabney** is an Oprah Winfrey Scholar who is passionate about education and poetry.

Kwame Sound Daniels is an artist based out of Maryland. Xir first book, *Light Spun*, is out with *Perennial Press* in August 2022. Kwame's theatre reviews are on Richmond Theatre Critics Circle's website. Xe were a speaker at the Conference for Community Writing for the Artsies Mentorship Program. Xe are an Anaphora Arts Residency Fellow and are an MFA candidate for Vermont College of Fine Arts. Kwame learns plant medicine, paints, and pickles vegetables in xir spare time.

Jeanine DeHoney's writing can be found online, in anthologies, and magazines including *Essence*, *Beautiful Black*, *Today's Black Woman*, *Rigorous* magazine, *Wow: Women on Writing*, *Literary Mama*, *Soul In Space*, and *The Dirty Spoon Radio Hour and Journal*. Her poem won first place in the Colorism Healing Writing Anthology contest and her prose won first place in table/feast's The Blossom Contest. She has work forthcoming in anthologies from Black Lawrence Press and Black Freighter Press. Jeanine was named an Honor Award winner for Sleeping Bear Press, Own Voices Own Stories 2022 Award season and her picture book has been acquired for publication.

doris diosa davenport (pronouns: person / per): Performance poet, writer, educator & independent scholar; BA Paine College; MA SUNY/Buffalo, NY; PhD Univ. of So. Calif. Visionary 75-year-old born (Jan. 29, 1949) & raised in traditional Cherokee Homelands (aka Northeast Georgia). Sapiosexual lesbian-feminist; Member of CLA (cla-scholars.org), Alternate ROOTS (alternateroots.org) and The International (& *Intergalactic*) LGBTQ+ Nation! Per continually, adamantly works to end all forms of oppression, towards truth & honesty – based egalitarian, inclusive and *magical* realities. New book, *testimony: proclamations, poems, potions* is person's 13th published book. Contact: zorahpoet7@gmail.com. Believes in joy; therefore, VERY happy to be included here.

Whitney French is a writer, multidisciplinary artist, and publisher. She edited the anthology *Black Writers Matter* a collection of creative nonfiction, the winner of the Saskatchewan Book Award for Publishing 2020. As a Hurston Wright Foundation fellow, Whitney French is a self-described Black futurist, with writings in *ARC Poetry*, *GEIST*, *WATER Magazine*, *FIYAH* and *Quill and Quire*. She has lectured in a number of spaces including Spellman College, Wayne State University, Aga Khan Museum, and Howard University. French is now the co-founder and publisher of Hush Harbour, the only Black queer feminist press in Canada. Currently, she lives in Toronto.

Regina YC Garcia is an award-winning poet, language artist, and English professor. She received a BA from UNC-CH with a BA in speech communication with a concentration in oral interpretation of literature and ECU where she received an MAEd and Graduate Certificate in multicultural and transnational literature. Her work appears in The AutoEthnographer, The Amistad, Main Street Rag. Her work has also been featured in an Emmy winning episode of "Muse," as well as in the 2022 Sacred 9 Project of Tulane University. Her book, *The Firetalker's Daughter* from Finishing Line Press is due for release in March 2023.

Akua Lezli Hope is a creator and wisdom seeker using sound, words, fiber, glass, metal, & wire to create poems, patterns, stories, music, sculpture, adornments & peace. Her collections include *Embouchure: Poems on Jazz and Other Musics* (Writer's Digest award winner), *Them Gone, Otherwheres: Speculative Poetry* (2021 Elgin Award winner), & Stratospherics (@Quarantine Public Library). She edited *NOMBONO: An Anthology of Speculative Poetry by BIPOC Creators*, the history-making first (2021). A 3rd generation New Yorker, she exhibits her artwork, sings songs from her favorite Japanese anime, practices her soprano saxophone & prays for the cessation of suffering for all.

Regina Jamison lives in Brooklyn. She is a Lambda Literary 2014 Fellow. Her poetry has appeared online and in print in various literary journals such as *Switchgrass Review Journal*, *Mom Egg Review*, *Five Two One Magazine*, *Magma Literary Journal*, *Promethean Literary Journal*, and *Sinister Wisdom: Black Lesbian Revolution* among others. She was Guest Editor at *Gnashing Teeth Publishing* for *SHE: Seen. Heard. Engaged Anthology Vol. 1*. She has an MFA in creative writing. Her first novel, *Choosing Grace*, was published by Bella Books.

Yeva Johnson, a Pushcart Prize-nominated poet whose work appears in *Bellingham Review*, *Obsidian*, *sin cesar*, *Sinister Wisdom*, *When We Exhale Anthology*, *Yemassee*, and elsewhere, explores interlocking caste systems and possibilities for human co-existence in our biosphere. Yeva is a past Show Us Your Spines Artist-in-Residence

(RADAR Productions/SFPL), a Marion Weber Healing Arts Fellow at Mesa Refuge in 2022, a Brown Handler Resident, and poet in QTPOC4SHO, a San Francisco Bay Area artists' collective. Her debut chapbook, *Analog Poet Blues*, was published in 2023 by Nomadic Press/Black Lawrence Press.

Taylor King is originally from Birmingham, AL, and has lived in New Orleans since 2017. She recently graduated from the illustrious Xavier University of Louisiana with a B.A. in English. As a mother of one, Taylor is currently pursuing a master's degree in English with a concentration on African American literature at Texas Southern University. One of her favorite books is *Sula* by Toni Morrison. She loves to read, write poetry, and discuss all things literary with those around her.

Taylor Mckinnon (she/her) is a writer based in Boston, Massachusetts. She has a lifelong interest in poetry and has studied it in English, Latin, and Ancient Greek as an undergraduate and graduate student. She has been published in *A Gathering Together*. Currently in law school, Taylor is interested in the intersections of her identity as a Black woman living with disabilities and how the natural world shapes identity.

Jasminum McMullen's last three streams were Random Acts of Flyness, Poker Face, and Sleeping with the Enemy. Her writing has appeared in *Baby Teeth*, *midnight & indigo*, *Past Ten*, *A Gathering Together*, and forthcoming in *midnight & indigo*, and *Mamas, Martyrs, and Jezebel's* (Black Lawrence Press). She holds an MFA from Vermont College of Fine Arts. She lives in the Chicagoland area with her wife and senior pets.

Penny Mickelbury has been writing professionally for most of her adult life, first as a newspaper, radio, and television reporter, and for the past 30+ years as a playwright and novelist. For almost a dozen years Penny was writing three separate mystery series at the same time: The *Carol Ann Gibson* legal series; the *Gianna Maglione/Mimi Patterson* police and journalist series; and the *Phil Rodriquez PI* series. She has seen 14 novels and a collection of short stories published, and she has contributed stories to several collections. Her newest and 16th novel, *Two Wings To Hide My Face*, publishes December 5, 2023, is the sequel to 2019's well-received *Two Wings To Fly Away*.

Marlee Alcina Miller (she/they) is a multidisciplinary artist with a special focus on writing and performance. Her work explores the dreamscape, love in all its many forms, and radical vulnerability. She attributes a large part of her artistic influence to dancing with her queer chosen family, Audre Lorde, writing her signature love letters, and her ancestral lineage. Marlee Alcina is currently pursuing an MFA in narrative nonfiction at the University of Georgia. She is the author of *Mommy Issues; Poems for the Fragile, Queer Heart*. Their writing has also appeared in previous issues of *Sinister Wisdom: A Multicultural Lesbian Literary & Art Journal*.

Sienna L. M. is a 2022-2023 Artist Support Grantee made possible by The North Carolina Arts Council, a state agency through the Pitt County Arts Council at Emerge; the 2022 Sims Library of Poetry bookmark contest winner; the 2021 Colorism Healing Writing Contest Guest Judge; a featured artist by *The Black Light Project* in 2021, and a contributing author to publications like *Black Nerds Create*, *Cocoa Butter & Hair Grease*, *Black Oak Society*, *midnight & indigo*, and *Black Minds Mag*. Sienna is professionally developing her literary artistry through her advantageous membership with The North Carolina Writers' Network.

Elizabeth Mudenyo is a Scarborough-raised poet, community-engaged artist and arts manager. Elizabeth is a fellow of The Watering Hole and the Poetry Incubator. She was a participant of the Hurston/Wright Poetry Weekend with Danez Smith and Diaspora Dialogues Short Form Mentorship. Her work has appeared in *Write Magazine*, *Arc Magazine*, *carte-blanche*, *Canthius*, *CV2*, and elsewhere. She is an MFA Candidate at the University of Guelph. Her poetry chapbook, *With Both Hands*, is available through Anstruther Press. elizabethmudenyo.com

Laura Doyle Péan (they/them) is a 23-year-old queer Haitian-Quebecois multidisciplinary artist, poet and activist who is committed to social justice and fascinated by the relationship between art and movement work. Laura published their first book, *Cœur Yoyo*, in 2020, and has participated in many artistic productions with the queer feminist collective Les Allumeuses. Laura's work is featured in multiple Quebec literary publications (*Lettres Québécoises*, *Estuaire*, *Zinc*, *XYZ*), and has been presented in art projects in Belgium, France, Mexico, Russia, and the UK. The English translation of their book, *Yo-yo Heart*, came out in London last October, with the 87 press.

Tiffany Smalls received her BA in creative writing from SUNY Potsdam. Currently residing in Rome, New York, she divides her time between being a coordinator at the Turning Stone Casino, working on her latest musical, *Day and Age*, and making handcrafted jewelry. Her work has appeared in publications by Paragon Press,

Firewords Magazine, *Beatific Magazine*, *The Haberdasher*, *Poets' Choice*, and *Genre: Urban Arts*. She is thrilled to have an opportunity to share her work with the world.

Patrick Sylvain is a poet, writer, social, and literary critic. Twice nominated for the Pushcart Prize. Published in several creative anthologies, journals, periodicals, and reviews including: *African American Review*, *Agni, American Poetry Review, Callaloo, The Caribbean Writer, Chicago Quarterly Review*, *Ep;phany*, *Magma Poetry*, *Ploughshares*, and *Prairie Schooner*. Sylvain has degrees from the University of Massachusetts (B.A.), Harvard University (Ed.M.), Boston University (MFA), and Brandeis University (PhD). Sylvain is an assistant professor at Simmons University, and he is also on faculty at Harvard University's History and Literature Division. Sylvain's poetry chapbook, *Underworlds*, is published by Central Square Press (2018). Sylvain is a featured poet on Benjamin Boone's Poetry and Jazz CD *The Poets are Gathering* (Oct 2020), and he is the leading author of *Education Across Borders: Immigration, Race, and Identity in the Classroom* (Beacon Press, Feb 2022).

Audrey Williams is an international writer, certified medium, spiritual teacher, and the published author of poetry, short stories, essays, and articles. Her work has appeared in *African American Review*, *Verse/Chorus*, *Anthology*, *Hauntings: An Anthology*, *borrowed solace*, *Bewildering Stories*, *Torrid Literature*, *Pay Attention Journal*, *The National Summit Magazine*, and other journals. She earned her MFA from Chicago State University. Acknowledgments to Kelvin, Chad, Danielle, Chris, Jeremy, Malik, London, and Kairo.

Shawn Williams is a VCU alumna who earned their Bachelors in African-American studies & English. Utilizing their experiences as a queer Afro-Latine and Vietnamese scholar, Shawn writes and crafts narratives that challenge and critique our thoughts around the personal as political, Black transfeminism, and interpreting Black musical performance in identity-making. Shawn is an active member of the Richmond, Virginia community; hosting donation drives, letter writing groups, and Black student wellness events. Through their coalition building in and outside the university, they seek to follow in other Africana students' footsteps in their will and self-determination towards collective liberation.

www.ingramcontent.com/pod-product-compliance
Lightning Source LLC
Chambersburg PA
CBHW031001210726
48290CB00007B/2409